T0214391

SpringerBriefs in Computer Science

More information about this series at http://www.springer.com/series/10028

Xinyuan Wang • Douglas Reeves

Traceback and Anonymity

 Springer

Xinyuan Wang
Department of Computer Science
George Mason University
Fairfax, VA, USA

Douglas Reeves
Department of Computer Science
North Carolina State University
Raleigh, NC, USA

ISSN 2191-5768 ISSN 2191-5776 (electronic)
SpringerBriefs in Computer Science
ISBN 978-1-4939-3439-3 ISBN 978-1-4939-3441-6 (eBook)
DOI 10.1007/978-1-4939-3441-6

Library of Congress Control Number: 2015953645

Springer New York Heidelberg Dordrecht London

Printed on acid-free paper

Springer Science+Business Media LLC New York is part of Springer Science+Business Media (www.
springer.com)

Contents

Chapter 1
Introduction

Cyber attack has become a top threat to our society. With more than one billion hosts [2] connected to the Internet, our society is becoming increasingly dependent on the Internet. Now the perpetrators have plenty choices of potential targets and they could attack the chosen Internet hosts from virtually anywhere in the world and cause damages to the victims.

For example, NASA has been under repeated attacks in the past few years, and its Jet Propulsion Lab has been found compromised [43]. In the recent data breach attack on Target, 40 million customers' credit and debit card information was stolen. In the recent cyber attack on Home Depot, 56 million shoppers' credit card information was compromised. A recent survey [62] showed that "the annual average cost per company of successful cyber attacks increased to $20.8 million in financial services, $14.5 million in the technology sector, and $12.7 million in communications industries."

In certain cases, cyber attacks could even cause the victim out of business. In June 2011, attackers compromised the information system of Dutch certificate authority DigiNotar, and generated over 500 fraudulent security certificates for high-profile Web sites such as Google, Facebook, Twitter, Microsoft and Skype. Such forged certificates could be used to impersonate Websites and intercept user information. A few monthly later, DigiNotar filed bankruptcy after the news broke about the security breach [40].

Besides financial motivations, cyber attacks such as hacktivism can be politically motivated. For example, it has been reported [41] that hackers have targeted bankers' personal data as a way to support the "Occupy Wall Street" movement. McAfee Predicted [42] that there will more such Hacktivism in 2012.

One major contributor to such growing threat of network-based attacks is the lack of attack attribution. Unlike the telephone systems, the Internet was never designed for tracking and tracing users' behavior. Most existing network security mechanisms such as firewalls [31], IPSEC [25] and IDS [5, 22] are focused on intrusion prevention and detection. However, even the perfect intrusion detection

© The Author(s) 2015

X. Wang, D. Reeves, *Traceback and Anonymity*, SpringerBriefs in Computer Science, DOI 10.1007/978-1-4939-3441-6_1

will not be able to tell where the detected attacks come from. What is missing from existing network security mechanisms is an effective way to identify network based intruders and hold them accountable for their intrusions.

Without effective intrusion source tracing and identification, those network based intruders have all the potential gains with virtually no risk of being caught. On the other hand, an effective and accurate attack tracing capability helps to eliminate network based attack from its root by identifying and catching those perpetrators responsible for the attack. From the attacker's point of view, if the risk of being caught and the consequent penalty are high enough compared with the potential gain of network based attack, he or she would be reluctant to attack again. Thus even an imperfect attack tracing capability could help to repel potential future attacks.

Because of the current Internet architecture, it is much easier for network based attackers to conceal their origin than for defenders to trace and identify their origin. To avoid being identified and tracked, attackers use all kinds of techniques to evade detection [37] and tracking. One common technique to conceal the attack source is to launder the attack through hosts of third party. Recent trend of cloud computing enables attackers to launch attacks from rented hosts from cloud provider. Specifically, recent attack on Sony's Playstation Network used rented hosts in Amazon EC2 [44]. All these would make it harder for the attack victim to find out the true source of the attacker after identifying the attack. Consequently, there is a pressing need to develop a capability for identifying the source of detected attacks. Network based attack can not be effectively repelled or eliminated until its source is known.

Besides the needs of traceback, there are legitimate reasons to keep certain online activities anonymous. For example, to encourage candid expression of opinions, an online survey may want to keep each response anonymous. In addition, people may want to keep their online activities private and do not want others know from where they browse the Internet and what web sites they visit. To help provide the anonymity and privacy to certain online activities, various anonymity systems have been developed and deployed. Specifically, Tor [17] and Anonymizer [3] use intermediate proxies and encryption to anonymize user's internet traffic.

The goal of anonymity system is exactly the opposite to that of traceback in that it aims to remove or conceal the true identity of the user or his/her Internet activity. While anonymity system helps protect the privacy and anonymity of legitimate online activities, they can also be abused by perpetrators to disguise the source of their attacks. For example, attackers can easily launder their attacks through low-latency anonymous network such as Tor, anonymizer before attacking the final targets. Therefore, it is necessary to understand how effective existing anonymity techniques are and whether we can "break" through existing anonymity systems in order to trace the attackers behind anonymity systems.

In this paper, we want to leave the controversy about the traceback and anonymity aside, and focus on the technical aspects of achieving traceback and anonymity. Specifically, we want to investigate the interaction between traceback and anonymity, and we want to understand the fundamental limitation of both traceback and low-latency anonymity systems.

The rest of this paper is organized as the following. Chapter 2 formulates the traceback problem. Chapter 3 describes existing approaches in traceback. Chapter 4 presents active timing based traceback approaches and the countermeasures against such active timing based approaches. Chapter 5 formulates the anonymity problem. Chapter 6 investigates fundamental limitations in low-latency anonymity systems. Chapter 7 concludes the paper.

Chapter 2
The Traceback Problem

In this chapter, we model the network based attacks and formulate the traceback problem to be studied.

2.1 Network-Based Attack

We refer to network-based attack as the process or event that an attacker sends out attack packets from an attacker host, through the network, to one or more victim hosts (or target hosts) and causes damage.

When attack packets reach the attack target, one important clue about the attack source is the source IP address of attack packet. However, the source IP address of attack packet is usually not the attack source as most attacks take advantage of one or more anonymity techniques to hide their origin.

One frequently used technique to hide the attack source is to simply spoof the source IP address of the attack packets [58]. Because IP routing is based on the destination address only, the attack packets can be transmitted to the attack target with virtually any source address. This kind of source address spoofing has been widely used in various denial-of-service attacks as the attacker expects no response traffic from the attack target. For attacks with bi-directional communications such as classic break-in type of intrusion [56], source address spoofing is difficult to be used because the attacker may not see the response traffic sent from the attack target back to the spoofed IP address.

Another technique to disguise the attack source is by"staging" the attack packets through some intermediate hosts or systems. For example, the attack traffic may pass through a number of intermediate hosts, $H_1, \ldots, H_n$, before attacking the final target. The intermediate hosts will forward the attack traffic with some transformation. Figure 2.1 depicts one example of the transformations at an intermediate host. The reception of packet P_i at time t_i causes H_i to generate and

© The Author(s) 2015

X. Wang, D. Reeves, *Traceback and Anonymity*, SpringerBriefs
in Computer Science, DOI 10.1007/978-1-4939-3441-6_2

Fig. 2.1 Packet transformation when forwarded through intermediate host

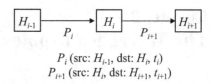

$$P_i \text{ (src: } H_{i-1}, \text{ dst: } H_i, t_i)$$
$$P_{i+1} \text{ (src: } H_i, \text{ dst: } H_{i+1}, t_{i+1})$$

send out a new packet P_{i+1} to H_{i+1} at time t_{i+1}. When packet P_i reaches H_i from H_{i-1}, it has source address H_{i-1}, destination address H_i. Now packet P_{i+1} has source address H_i and destination address H_{i+1}. Furthermore, the packet content of P_{i+1} could be transformed from that of P_i. For example, P_i from H_{i-1} to H_i could be a telnet packet and P_{i+1} from H_i to H_{i+1} could be a SSH packet. One invariant relation between packets P_i and P_{i+1} of the same attack traffic is the causality relation: the arrival of packet P_i at H_i at one time somehow causes H_i to generate and send out packet P_{i+1} to a new destination at a later time. However, the causality between packet P_i and packet P_{i+1} becomes difficult to recognize when the delay between the two packets is large.

Depending on the characteristics of forwarding and transformation, intermediate staging hosts along the attack path could be classified into three categories: (1) *stepping-stone*, (2) *zombie*, and (3) *reflector*. A stepping-stone [69] is a host controlled (e.g., compromised or rented) by the attacker which acts as a bidirectional-conduit for the attack traffic. The stepping-stone supports real-time bidirectional communication and it usually introduces very small delay. While the content of the packets could be changed drastically (by encryption for example), the essence of the packet content remains the same across the stepping-stone. Because stepping-stone supports bi-directional, interactive communications while conceals the source of the communication, it is frequently used in intrusion type of attacks. Classic penetration attack [56] usually comes through multiple stepping-stones.

A zombie host is a host controlled (e.g., compromised or rented) by the attacker that is used as an attack launching point when triggered by the attacker. The trigger of the attack traffic from the zombie could be some special packet sent by the attacker or a Trojan or logic bomb previously planted by the attacker into the zombie host. The zombie is unidirectional and the attack triggering traffic and the triggered attack traffic are usually fundamentally different. For example, a single ping packet from the attacker to the zombie could trigger an enormous amount of essentially different attack traffic sent from zombie further to the target. The attacker could also plant into the zombie some logical bomb timed to execute minutes, hours or even days later. All these make it very difficult to identify the trigger of the attack traffic. This kind of zombie hosts has been widely used in distributed denial-of-service (DDoS) attacks.

Unlike stepping-stone and zombie host, a reflector is a host not controlled by the attacker but somehow has been tricked to take part in the attack in an innocent manner that is consistent with its normal operation. For example, the attacker could send some host with ICMP request packet devised with attack target's address as its source address. Upon reception of such ICMP request, the host would think it comes

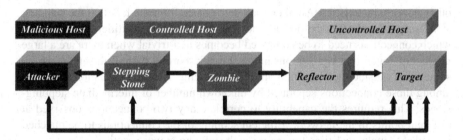

Fig. 2.2 The overall model of network based attack

from the attack target, and it would send the ICMP reply to the attack target. In such a way, the uncompromised host acts as the reflector of the attack traffic. When the attacker tricks many such reflectors into sending ICMP reply packets to one target, that target could be flooded. "Smurf" [60] is a well-known DDoS attack that utilizes an ICMP reflector to flood the target.

Figure 2.2 illustrates the overall model of network-based attack that uses various techniques to disguise the real source of the attack. The double arrowed line represents bi-directional connection and the single arrowed line denotes one-way communication. Generally, zombie and reflector can only be used in unidirectional attack (i.e. denial of service attack [58–60]). Stepping-stone, however, could be used in both bi-directional, interactive break-in type of intrusions and unidirectional flooding type of attacks.

The overall traceback problem of network-based attacks has two distinct sub-problems: (1) how to identify the real source of the packet with spoofed source address; (2) how to identify the causality of traffic into and out of a given intermediate host (or equivalently to identify which incoming flow, if there is any, causes a particular outgoing flow).

For the first sub-problem, IP traceback techniques [4, 15, 20, 33, 49, 54] have been developed to trace packets with spoofed source address. However, IP traceback could not identify the causality of traffic through intermediate host thus it could not trace through intermediate hosts. For example, when attack traffic originating from host A is forwarded by host B toward host C, the victim at host C can use IP traceback technique to find the attack traffic comes from host B (even if the attack traffic from B to C has a spoofed source address). But IP traceback techniques could not determine that the attack traffic from B to C actually originated from host A. In order to trace through the intermediate host B, we need techniques that could identify which, if any, incoming flow into host B causes the attack flow from B to C.

Since the stepping stone acts merely as a bidirectional conduit, it will send out the packets it has received after some transformation has been performed. Therefore the identification of the causality of connections through a stepping-stone could be achieved by matching the incoming connections with outgoing connections of the stepping-stone. We refer this matching as the correlation of connections. One major challenge in the correlation is that the connections may be transformed in content or other flow characteristics. Another challenge comes from the fact that the stepping stone may be unknown before any correlation has been identified. Determining which connections need to be compared becomes non-trivial when there are a large number of concurrent connections in the network. Further more if the attack passes some hosts outside the observing area of the tracing system, correlation is needed among those connections separated by unknown number of intermediate stepping-stones. This requires the capability to correlate any two connections observed at different points in the network. Efficient scoping of the connections to be matched is needed to make real-time tracing through stepping-stones practical.

In this work, we focus on addressing how to trace the interactive bidirectional attack traffic through intermediate hosts such as stepping-stones at real-time. Ideally a tracing system, as a solution to the traceback problem, would be able to identify the person who is responsible for the attack. However, the identification or authentication of a user of a machine will not be addressed here as it is a generic problem that is not specific to traceback. In this research, the traceback problem is limited to determining the source host of the network-based attacks.

2.2   Overall Traceback Model

In this work, we refer to one network communication between two hosts in the Internet as one connection. The host that originates the connection is called the source host, and the host that terminates the connection is called the destination host. The connections that originate from one host are called the outgoing connections of the host, and the connections that terminate at one host are called the incoming connections of the host. One host may have multiple outgoing connections and multiple incoming connections at the same time. In the Internet environment, a connection consists of a number of packets between the source host and the destination hosts, and it could be either unidirectional or bidirectional. Each packet in a connection has at least one header and optional payload, and each packet has a departure time from the source host and arrival time at the destination host. Generally, a connection can also be called flow, which can be uniquely identified by tuple

$$\langle \text{Source IP, Source Port, Destination IP, Destination Port, Protocol} \rangle$$

Given a series of computer hosts $H_1, H_2, \ldots H_{n+1}$ ($n > 1$), when a person (or a program) sequentially connects from H_i into H_{i+1} ($i = 1, 2, \ldots n$), we refer to the sequence of connections $\langle c_1, c_2, \ldots c_n \rangle$, where $c_i = \langle H_i, H_{i+1} \rangle$ ($i = 1, \ldots n$), as a connection chain on $\langle H_1, H_2, \ldots H_{n+1} \rangle$, and intermediate hosts $H_2, \ldots H_n$ as stepping stones. Here connection c_i terminated at host H_{i+1} causes another connection c_{i+1} outgoing from host H_{i+1} and host H_{i+1} essentially forwards the traffic of c_i to c_{i+1}. All c_i's are always distinct, but not all H_i's are always distinct. In case some host appears more than once in sequence $\langle H_1, H_2, \ldots H_{n+1} \rangle$, there exists loop in the connection chain $\langle c_1, c_2, \ldots c_n \rangle$.

The tracing problem of a connection chain through stepping stones is, given c_n of some unknown connection chain $\langle c_1, c_2, \ldots c_n \rangle (n > 1)$, to identify $\langle c_1, c_2, \ldots c_n \rangle$.

Any particular connection chain $\langle c_1, c_2, \ldots c_n \rangle$ is a sequence of connections. We refer those connections within the same connection chain as correlated to each other and the corresponding set $\{c_1, c_2, \ldots c_n\}$ as the set of correlated connections or correlation set. This can be formally modelled by a binary relation on the overall connection set. Let $\hat{C}$ represent all connections being examined, we define binary relation CORR on the overall connection set $\hat{C}$ such that

$$\forall c, c' \in \hat{C}(c \text{ CORR } c' \text{ iff } (c \in \{c_1, c_2, \ldots c_n\} \Rightarrow c' \in \{c_1, c_2, \ldots c_n\})) \qquad (2.1)$$

It is obvious that CORR is specific to the correlation set and it is (1) self-reflexive; (2) symmetric and (3) transitive. Therefore binary relation CORR is an equivalence relation on $\hat{C}$ and it partitions the overall set of connections into a particular set of correlated connections and else.

Because connection chain $\langle c_1, c_2, \ldots c_n \rangle$ is a sequence of connections, each c_i has a unique order number $\text{Ord}(c_i)$ associated with it. The overall ordering information of $\langle c_1, c_2, \ldots c_n \rangle$ can be formally modelled by the binary relation $\prec$ on $\{c_1, c_2, \ldots c_n\}$ such that

$$\forall c, c' \in \{c_1, c_2, \ldots c_n\}(c \prec c' \text{ iff } \text{Ord}(c) < \text{Ord}(c')) \qquad (2.2)$$

It is obvious that $\prec$ well orders set $\{c_1, c_2, \ldots c_n\}$ and it uniquely determines $\langle c_1, c_2, \ldots c_n \rangle$ from $\{c_1, c_2, \ldots c_n\}$.

For any particular connection chain $\langle c_1, c_2, \ldots c_n \rangle$, there exists unique binary relation CORR and $\prec$, which in turn uniquely determines $\langle c_1, c_2, \ldots c_n \rangle$. Therefore, the overall tracing problem of stepping stone can be divided into the following sub-problems:

- **Correlation Problem:** Given c_n of some unknown connection chain $\langle c_1, c_2, \ldots c_n \rangle$, identify set $\{c_1, c_2, \ldots c_n\}$; Or equivalently, given any two connections c and c', determine if c CORR c'.
- **Serialization Problem:** Given a set of correlated connections $C = \{c_1, c_2, \ldots c_n\}$; and some information about the relative order of correlated connections, serialize $\{c_1, c_2, \ldots c_n\}$; into a sequence $\langle c'_1, c'_2, \ldots c'_n \rangle (c'_i \in C, i = 1, \ldots n)$ such that $c'_i \prec c'_{i+1} (i = 1, \ldots n - 1)$; Or equivalently, given any two connections c and c', determine if $c \prec c'$ or $c' \prec c$.

The result of solution for the correlation problem is an unordered set of connections and the result of solution for the serialization problem is a sequence of connections. It is easy to see that the solution of the serialization problem is based upon the result of the correlation problem solution. Therefore, the correlation problem has to be solved first in order to solve the overall tracing problem of stepping stones.

2.2.1   Correlation Problem Solution Model

Given binary relation CORR, we can define corresponding *correlation function CF*:
$\hat{C} \times \hat{C} \to \{0, 1\}$ such that:

$$CF(c, c') = \begin{cases} 1, & \text{if } c \text{ CORR } c' \\ 0, & \text{otherwise} \end{cases} \tag{2.3}$$

Therefore the correlation problem can be equivalently expressed as: given any two connections c and c', find correlation function CF such that $CF(c, c') = 1$ *iff* c CORR c'.

In practice, the correlation analysis is based on some unique and invariant characteristics (e.g., content, header information, inter-packet timing)of the connections. We model such connection characteristics via a *metric function* of the connection

$$M : \hat{C} \times P \to Z \tag{2.4}$$

where $\hat{C}$ is the set of connections or flows to be correlated, P is some domain of parameters that may impact the choice of metrics to be used in correlation and Z is the connection metric domain that represent the connection characteristics to be used for correlation.

Based on connection metric, we define the *correlation value function (CVF)* as

$$CVF : Z \times Z \times \delta \to \{0, 1\} \tag{2.5}$$

where δ is some threshold.[1] The result of *CVF* is either 0 or 1 indicating whether the two connections are detected to be correlated based on their corresponding correlation metric and threshold δ.

In other word, connections c and c' are considered correlated *iff*

$$CVF(M(c, p), M(c', p), \delta) = 1 \tag{2.6}$$

Therefore the correlation problem is now translated to: *find or construct M, p, CVF and δ such that*

$$\forall c_i \in \{c_1, \ldots c_n\} \forall c \in \hat{C}[CVF(M(c_i, p), M(c, p), \delta) = 1 \text{ iff } c \in \{c_1, \ldots c_n\}] \tag{2.7}$$

The key to find effective *M, p, CVF* and δ is to identify some defining characteristics of connections that are both unique and invariant across routers and stepping-stones. Specifically, unique characteristics of connections allow us

---

[1]Depending on the metric function M and parameter P, threshold δ can be real value, integer or other appropriate form.

to effectively distinguish one connection from other uncorrelated connections and correlate only those really related flows together. In case the original connections do not have unique enough correlation characteristics, we could slightly adjust some characteristic of the original connections to make their correlation metric more unique to enable more effective correlation.

2.3 Evaluation Criteria of Traceback

According to the overall tracing problem model, both correlation and serialization problems can be modelled as detection problem – determining if certain property exists or not. Therefore, the stepping stone tracing and correlation approaches can be evaluated by the generic detection problem evaluation criteria.

Assume p is the property to be detected. Let S denote the whole space in which property p could be true, let P denote the space within S in which property p is true, and let T denote the space within S that the detector reports positive of property p. Therefore $T \subseteq S, T + \neg T = S, P \subseteq S$, and $P + \neg P = S$. Figure 2.3 illustrates the relations between S, T and P. A perfect detector would generate T exact the same as P, and a less than perfect detector would generate T that either misses part of P or mistakenly includes part of $\neg P$.

Set of $T \cap P$ is considered *true positive* (TP), set of $T \cap \neg P$ is considered *false positive* (FP), set of $\neg T \cap P$ is considered false negative (FN) and set of $\neg T \cap \neg P$ is considered *true negative* (TN). A TP indicates the case that a positive detection is actually correct in that the property p exists. A FP indicates the case that a positive detection is actually wrong in that the property p does not exist.

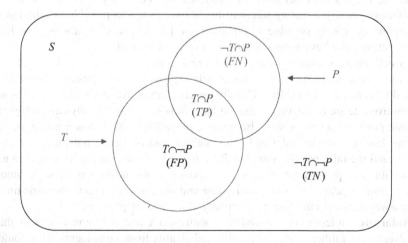

Fig. 2.3 Venn diagram of detection problem

The conditional probability $\Pr(T|P) = \Pr(T \cap P)/\Pr(P)$ is considered as *true positive rate* (TPR), which represents the probability of positive detection assuming the property p exists. The TPR quantitatively expresses the "completeness" of the detector. In Fig. 2.3, the TPR is represented by the ratio between area of $T \cap P$ and area of P.

The conditional probability $\Pr(T|\neg P) = \Pr(T \cap \neg P)/\Pr(\neg P)$ is considered as *false positive rate* (FPR), which represents the probability of positive detection assuming the property p does not exist. The FPR quantitatively express the "soundness" of the detector. In Fig. 2.3, the FPR is represented by the ratio between area of $T \cap \neg P$ and area of $\neg P$.

The conditional probability $\Pr(\neg T|P) = \Pr(\neg T \cap P)/\Pr(P)$ is considered as *false negative rate* (FNR), which represents the probability of negative detection assuming the property p exists. In Fig. 2.3, the FNR is represented by the ratio between area of $\neg T \cap P$ and area of P.

The conditional probability $\Pr(\neg T|\neg P) = \Pr(\neg T \cap \neg P)/\Pr(\neg P)$ is considered as *true negative rate* (FNR), which represents the probability of negative detection assuming the property p does not exist. In Fig. 2.3, the TNR is represented by the ratio between area of $\neg T \cap \neg P$ and area of $\neg P$.

It is easy to see that TPR + FNR $= 1$ and FPR + TNR $= 1$. Therefore we only need to consider correlation true positive rate and correlation false positive rate when assess a correlation solution.

The solution of tracing problem can be evaluated by the following criteria:

- **Usability** is a measure of applicability of the tracing and correlation system, which usually includes (1) assumptions of the attacks; (2) required information for tracing; (3) limitation of the tracing system; and (4) overhead introduced. For example, some tracing approach needs sustained steady packet streams to be useful, while some other tracing approaches may need only a few packets to be effective. Ideally, a tracing solution should have as few as possible assumptions, require as few as possible information for tracing, have as few as possible limitations, and have as few as possible overhead to be effective.
- **Effectiveness** measures how effective and correct the tracing can be under various conditions. It can be quantitatively expressed by true positive rate (TPR) and false positive rate (FPR). Usually the correlation true positive rate and false positive rate are conflicting in that higher true positive rate usually causes higher false positive rate and lower false positive rate usually causes lower true positive rate. Each correlation solution has an inherent tradeoff between the true positive rate and the false positive rate. Ideally, a tracing solution should have as high as possible true positive rate and as low as possible false positive at the same time. The limit of achievable true positive rate and false positive rate at the same time in a way measures the inherent difficulty of the tracing problem.
- **Robustness** refers to the capability to withstand active countermeasures by the adversary to further disguise its source and identity from being identified. It could be quantitatively expressed by the countermeasure's negative impact over the

tracing and correlation effectiveness. Ideally, the adverse impact of adversary's countermeasures over the true positive and false positive rates of a robust tracing solution should be minimal.

- **Stealthiness** measures to what extend the tracing can be conducted without being detected by the adversary.

Chapter 3
Existing Approaches in Traceback

3.1 Classification of Traceback Approaches

Based on source of tracing or correlation information, the traceback and correlation approaches can be divided into two categories: host-based and network-based. Host-based approaches rely on information collected at the hosts that are used for stepping stones. Such information includes user login activity, new arrival of connections and new initiation of connections to other hosts. Network-based approaches use some characteristics of network connections and exploit the property of network connections: the essence or semantics of the application level content of connections is invariant across stepping stones.

Based on how the traffic is traced, tracing approaches can further be classified into either active or passive. In particular, passive approaches passively monitor and compare all the traffic all the time and they do not scope the traffic to be traced. On the other hand, active approaches may actively but slightly change some characteristics of selected packets in order to make the packet flow easier to identify and correlate. Furthermore, active approaches could dynamically control when, where, what and how the traffic is to be correlated through customized packet processing, and they only trace "interested" traffic when needed. Table 3.1 provides a classification of representative existing correlation and tracing approaches.

The fundamental problem of host-based tracing approach is that it requires the participation of each stepping stones and it places its trust upon those monitored stepping stones themselves. In specific, the host-based tracing approach depends on the correlation of connections at every stepping stone in the intrusion connection chain. If one stepping stone provides misleading correlation information, the whole tracing system is fooled. On the other hand, network-based approach does not require participation of stepping stones, nor does it place its trust on the monitored stepping stones. It only requires the information about the connections to and from stepping stones.

© The Author(s) 2015

X. Wang, D. Reeves, *Traceback and Anonymity*, SpringerBriefs
in Computer Science, DOI 10.1007/978-1-4939-3441-6_3

Table 3.1 Classification of traceback approaches

	Passive	Active
Host-based	DIDS, CIS, STOP	
Network-based	Thumprinting, ON/OFF-based, deviation-based	IDIP, SWT, IPD-based

The earliest work on connection correlation was host-based which tracks the users' login activity at different hosts. Later work has been network-based that exploits different characteristics of network connections. The earlier network-based approaches relied on comparing the packet contents of the connections to be correlated, and recent network-based approaches have focused on the timing characteristics of connections, in order to correlate encrypted connections (i.e. traffic encrypted using IPSEC [25] or SSH [66]).

3.2   Traceback of Unencrypted Attack Traffic

The tracing and correlating of unencrypted connections through stepping stones have been studied since the earliest works on the tracing problem of stepping stones. Notable works include: Distributed Intrusion Detection System (DIDS) [53], Caller Identification System (CIS) [24], Thumbprinting [55], Intrusion Detection and Isolation Protocol (IDIP) [50], Session TOken Protocol (STOP) [9].

In the rest of this section, we review and evaluate these works.

3.2.1   Distributed Intrusion Detection System (DIDS)

Distributed Intrusion Detection System (DIDS) [53] developed at UC Davis was designed to address the intrusion detection problem in LAN environment. To the best of our knowledge, it is the first work that tracks users' login activity across network. DIDS uses a host-based distributed architecture to keep track of all the users in the LAN through so-called NID (Network-user Identification) and account for all activities to network-wide intrusion detection systems. Each monitored host in the DIDS domain collects audit trails and sends audit abstracts to a centralized DIDS director for analysis. Besides the inherent limitations of host-based tracing approach, DIDS is limited to tracking users' login activity across the LAN through normal login within the DIDS domain. Furthermore, because of its centralized monitoring of network activities, it seems not feasible in large-scale network such as the Internet.

3.2.2   Caller Identification System (CIS)

The Caller Identification System (CIS) [24] is another host-based tracing mechanism. It eliminates centralized control by utilizing a distributed model. In CIS, each host assumes each remote user who tries to login has a connection chain, and each host keeps record about its view of the login chain for each logged in user. When the user from host H_{n-1} attempts to login into the host H_n, H_n asks H_{n-1} about its view of the login chain of that user, which should be $H_1, H_2, \ldots H_{n-1}$ ideally. After getting the login chain information from H_{n-1}, H_n queries each host in the login chain (ideally $H_1, H_2, \ldots H_{n-1}$) about their views of the login chain for the user who tries to login into H_n. Only when the login chain information from all queried hosts matches, will the login be granted at host H_n. Besides the inherent limitations of host-based approach, CIS introduces excessive overheard to the normal login process by requesting and reviewing information from every hosts along the login chain. In addition, CIS requires the capability to correlate incoming connection and outgoing connection at each stepping stone, which was not available when CIS was proposed. Later work of STOP [9] recognized this and tried to provide a way to determine the correlation of incoming and outgoing connections at a host.

3.2.3   Thumbprinting

Thumbprinting [55] is the first published network-based correlation technique. It utilizes a small quantity of information (called thumbprint) to summarize a certain section of a connection. The thumbprint is built, through principle component analysis technique in statistics, upon the frequencies that each character occurs within a period of time. Ideally it can distinguish a connection from unrelated connections and correlate a connection with those related connections in the same connection chain. Because it correlates based on connection content, thumbprinting works even when all stepping stones are compromised and under attacker's total control, and it can be useful when only part of the Internet implements thumbprinting. However, thumbprinting depends on clock synchronization to match the thumbprints of corresponding intervals of connections, and it is vulnerable to packet retransmission variation. One area that thumbprinting has not addressed is how to determine which connections are to be thumbprinted and how to determine which thumbprint should be matched with which thumbprint in order to find correlated connections.

3.2.4   Intrusion Detection and Isolation Protocol (IDIP)

IDIP (Intrusion Identification and Isolation Protocol) [50] is a proposal by Boeing's Dynamic Cooperating Boundary Controllers Program that uses an active approach to trace the incoming path and source of intrusion. In the proposal, special gateways called boundary controllers collaboratively locate and block the intruder by exchanging intrusion detection information, namely, attack descriptions. If the distributed boundary controllers are able to detect the ongoing attack described by the attack description, IDIP could identify the ongoing attack path by querying appropriate boundary controllers. While it does not require any boundary controller to record any connections for correlation, its intrusion tracing is closely coupled with intrusion detection. The effectiveness of IDIP depends on the effectiveness of intrusion identification through the attack description at each boundary controller. Therefore IDIP requires each boundary controller to have the same intrusion detection capability as the IDS at the intrusion target host. It is questionable whether the intermediate boundary controller is able to identify an intrusion at real-time based on a hard-coded attack description.

3.2.5 Session Token Protocol (STOP)

Session Token Protocol (STOP) [9] aims to find the mapping between the incoming and outgoing connections at a host. It is based upon the Identification Protocol (ident) defined in RFC1413, which enables the server side of a TCP connection to ask the client side about the process and corresponding UID that initiated the TCP connection. STOP extends the Identification Protocol by allowing the host to save application-level data about the process and user that opened the connection, and to send request to other host recursively. By saving and examining information about processes that originate the outgoing connection or terminate the incoming connection, STOP tries to map an incoming connection to a host with an outgoing connection from the host. However, there are few fundamental flaws in the design of STOP that severely limits its usability. First, STOP is a host-based protocol whose functionality depends on the correct information collected at the stepping stone itself. As the attacker is usually assumed to have total control over the stepping stone, he can easily kill or replace the STOP daemon running at the stepping stone, which would completely defeat the STOP system. Second, even if the STOP daemon is not touched by the attacker, it is still not guaranteed to provide the mapping between the incoming and outgoing connections at a host. This is because one process in a host could open multiple sockets and handles multiple incoming connections concurrently. Therefore, even if the STOP could find the process P and its corresponding UID that opened an outgoing connection Co, it may not be able to determine which one of the multiple incoming connections handled by process P should be mapped to the outgoing connection Co. In other word, STOP only works when (1) every stepping stone runs STOP daemon; and (2) no STOP daemon at each stepping stone is stopped or replaced by the attacker; and (3) each process that relays connections at each stepping stone opens only one incoming connection and one outgoing connections. In summary, it is questionable how useful the STOP would be in real-work situations.

3.2.6 Sleepy Watermark Tracing (SWT)

Sleepy Watermark Tracing (SWT) [65] is an active traffic correlation and tracing approach that leverages steganography techniques. By injecting unique and humanly invisible random strings to the traffic echoed back to the attacker, SWT is able to correlate and trace unencrypted traffic across stepping stones within a single keystroke by the intruder. By actively generating tracing traffic, it can correlate and trace even when the attack flow is idle (i.e., no keystroke from the intruder). Like all other content-based correlation approaches, SWT is only effective in tracing unencrypted traffic.

3.3 Traceback of Encrypted Attack Traffic

As the connection encryption tools (such as IPSEC and SSH) have been widely deployed, network based attackers can easily encrypt their attack connections when passing stepping stones. To address this new challenge, recent research work on the stepping stones tracing problem has been focused on how trace and correlate encrypted connections through stepping stones.

3.3.1 ON/OFF Based Approach

The ON/OFF based correlation [69] by Zhang and Paxson is the first network-based correlation scheme that utilizes the inter-packet timing characteristics to correlate interactive connections across stepping-stones. Depending on whether there is any traffic for a (adjustable) period of time, the duration of a flow can be divided into either ON of OFF periods. The correlation of two flows is based on mapping the ends of OFF periods (or equivalently the beginnings of ON periods). Because it correlates based on inter-packet timing characteristics rather than packet content, ON/OFF based correlation is able to correlate both encrypted and unencrypted connections, and it is robust against packet payload padding. However, ON/OFF based correlation requires that the packets of connections have precise, synchronized time stamps in order to be able to correlate them. This makes ON/OFF based correlation limited to detecting the correlation between only those connections that can be monitor at the same one point. And it is difficult or impractical for ON/OFF based correlation to correlate measurements taken at different points in the network.

3.3.2 Deviation Based Approach

The deviation-based approach [67] by Yoda and Etoh is another network-based correlation scheme. It defines the minimum average delay gap between the packet streams of two TCP connections as deviation. The deviation based approach considers both the packet timing characteristics and the TCP sequence numbers. It does not require clock synchronization and is able to correlate connections observed at different points of network. However, it can only correlate TCP connections that have one-to-one correspondences in their TCP sequence numbers, and thus is not able to correlate connections where padding is added to the packet payload (e.g. when certain types of encryptions are used).

The deviation based approach has been evaluated against several large network traces, and it has been shown that it is rare to have low deviation between random uncorrelated flows. This suggests that deviation based approach has low false positive rates. However, the published paper by Yoda and Etoh does not have evaluation on the correlation true positive rates.

3.3.3 IPD-Based Approach

In our early work [64], we have investigated if and how the inter-packet timing characteristics can be used to correlate both encrypted and unencrypted connections. Our experiments show that (after some filtering) inter-packet delays (IPDs) of both encrypted and unencrypted, interactive traffic are largely preserved across many hops and stepping stones. This enables correlation of encrypted traffic that has distinct inter-packet characteristics. We have found that normal interactive traffic such as telnet, SSH and rlogin are almost always distinctive enough to be correlated based on inter-packet delays. Since the IPD based approach depends on the existing IPDs of the traffic, it is not effective in correlating those traffic (e.g., file transfer) that do not have distinct inter-packet timing characteristics. As with any other passive approaches, IPD based approach is vulnerable to deliberate, active timing perturbation.

3.4 Tracing and Correlating Encrypted Connections with Timing Perturbation

Timing-based approaches have been shown to be able to correlate encrypted network flows. However, existing timing-based correlation approaches, are subject to countermeasures by the adversary. Specifically, the adversary can actively perturb the timing of network flows by adding deliberate delays to selected packets. Such timing perturbation could either make unrelated flows have similar timing characteristics, or make related flows exhibit different timing characteristics. Either case will adversely affect the effectiveness of any timing-based correlation. Therefore, it is very important to investigate how to make timing based correlation robust against timing perturbation.

3.4.1 Wavelet Based Approach

Donoho et al. [18] have investigated the theoretical limits on the attacker's ability to disguise his traffic through timing perturbation and packet padding (i.e., injection of bogus packets). By using a multiscale analysis technique, they are able to separate the long term behavior of the connection from the short term behavior of the connection, and they show that correlation from the long term behavior (of sufficiently long flows) is still possible despite timing perturbation by the attacker. However, they do not present any tradeoffs between the magnitude of the timing perturbation, the desired correlation effectiveness, and the number of packets needed. Another important issue that is not addressed by [18] is the correlation false positive rate. While the coarse scale analysis for long term behavior may filter out packet jitter introduced by the attacker, it could also filter out the inherent uniqueness and details of the flow timing. Therefore coarse scale analysis tends to increase the correlation false positive rate while increasing the correlation true positive rate of timing perturbed connections. Nevertheless, Donoho et al.'s work [18] represents a significant first step toward a better understanding of the inherent limitations of timing perturbation by the attacker on timing-based correlation. The important theoretical result is that correlation is still achievable for sufficiently long flows despite certain type of timing perturbations. What left open are the question whether correlation is achievable for arbitrarily distributed (rather than Pareto distribution conserving) random timing perturbation, and an analysis of the achievable tradeoff of the false positive and true positive rates.

3.5 Summary of Existing Traceback Approaches

The earliest work on the correlation of connections through stepping stones had focused on unencrypted connection and had been based on tracking users' login activities at different hosts [9, 24, 53]. Later work on correlation of unencrypted connections relied on comparing the packet contents of the connections to be correlated [55, 65].

To address the challenges introduced by the encryption of packets (i.e. traffic encrypted using IPSEC [25] or SSH [66]), recent works [64, 67, 69] have focused on utilizing the packet timing characteristics to correlate encrypted connections. As a result, timing based correlation approaches are vulnerable to the active timing perturbation by adversary.

To address the new challenges introduced by the active timing perturbation of encrypted connection, Donoho et al. [18] has used multi-scale analysis techniques to investigate the theoretical limits of active timing perturbation by attacker. They show that it is still possible to correlate the timing perturbed encrypted connections as long as the flow has enough packets.

We observe that previous approaches for tracing and correlating intrusion connections through stepping stones have substantial limitations and leave a number of fundamental questions open. In the following chapters, we address the limitations of existing traceback approaches and we describe our active timing based traceback approaches under various settings.

Chapter 4
Active Timing Based Traceback

As shown in Sect. 3.3, timing based correlation approaches are promising in correlating encrypted network flows. However, they are inherently sensitive to deliberate timing perturbation by the adversary. In particular, the adversary can increase the correlation false positive rate or decrease the correlation true positive rate by making unrelated flows have similar timing characteristics or making related flows exhibit different timing characteristics.

Compared with the active timing perturbation, the timing-based correlation approaches described in Sect. 3.3 are passive in that they simply measure existing, potentially perturbed inter-packet timing characteristics of network flows for correlation. Such a passive nature has put previous timing based correlation approaches at a disadvantage in front of active timing perturbation. As a result, passive timing based correlation approaches are vulnerable to active timing perturbation by the adversary, and they usually require a large number of packets in order to correlate in the presence of timing perturbation.

In this chapter, we focus on how to make timing base correlation probabilistically robust against active timing perturbation and seek to answer some fundamental questions regarding the achievable effectiveness and tradeoffs of timing-based correlation in the presence of active timing perturbation. To address the weakness of existing passive timing based correlation approaches, we propose using active approaches to counter the timing perturbation by the adversary. Specifically, we encode a unique watermark into the inter-packet timing of specified packet flows by slightly adjusting the timing of selected packets. The unique watermark encoded in the inter-packet timing of packet flow gives us a number of advantages over passive timing based approaches in the presence of timing perturbations by the adversary. First, unlike most existing passive timing based correlation approaches, our flow watermarking based correlation approaches do not make any limiting assumptions about (1) the distribution or random process of the original inter-packet timing of the packet flow to be correlated; (2) the distribution of random delays the adversary could add. Second, our methods require substantially less packets in the packet

© The Author(s) 2015
X. Wang, D. Reeves, *Traceback and Anonymity*, SpringerBriefs
in Computer Science, DOI 10.1007/978-1-4939-3441-6_4

flow in order to achieve the same level of correlation effectiveness of existing passive timing based correlation approaches. In theory, our flow watermarking based correlation can achieve arbitrarily close to 100 % true positive rate and arbitrarily close to 0 % false positive rate at the same time, despite arbitrarily large (but bounded) timing perturbation of arbitrary distribution by the adversary, as long as the packet flow is long enough and has sufficient packets.

4.1 Overall Flow Watermark Tracing Model

Based on the flow watermarking techniques, we can build flow watermark tracing system that exploits the observation that interactive connections (i.e. Telnet, SSH) are bidirectional. The key idea is to transparently watermark the backward traffic, from the attack target all the way back to the attacker, of the bidirectional attack connections. If the encoded watermark is both robust and unique, the watermarked traffic can be effectively correlated and traced across the network. As shown in Fig. 4.1, the attacker may launder through a number of hosts $(H_1, \ldots, H_n)$ before attacking the final target. Assuming the attacker has not gained full control of the attack target, the attack target will initiate the flow watermark tracing after it has detected the attack. Specifically, the attack target will transparently watermark the backward traffic of the bidirectional attack connection in the inter-packet timing, and notifies sensors across the network about the watermark. The sensors across the network will scan all the passing traffic for the presence of the specified watermark, and report to the target if it detects any flow that has the specified watermark.

Sensors can be deployed at various gateways, firewalls and edge routers across the network. Generally, the more sensors deployed, the better. However, how many sensors can be deployed in the network depend on not only the resource available but also the administrative privilege. How to optimally deploy limited number of sensors over particular network is an open research problem [38]. In this chapter, we leave aside the optimal sensor deployment issues, and instead focus on the flow watermarking approaches themselves.

Since we watermark the backward traffic at its very source – the attack target which is not controlled by the attacker, the attacker does have access to the

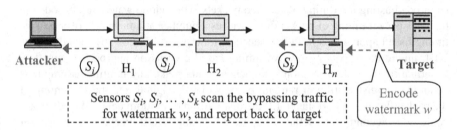

Fig. 4.1 Overall watermark tracing model

unwatermarked backward traffic. Therefore, it is very difficult for the attacker to determine exactly which packets have been delayed by the flow watermarking process.

We assume the following about the active timing perturbations by the adversary:

1. While the attacker can delay any or all packets of any packet flow that passes its node, the maximum delay is bounded.
2. The active timing perturbations by the adversary follow some distribution of finite variance and have the same covariance among each other.
3. The attacker does not drop or add any packets.[1]
4. While the flow watermarking scheme is public knowledge, the watermarking encoding and decoding parameters are shared secrets between the watermark encoder and the watermark detector(s).

Here we do not require that the packet order to be the kept same, as long as the total number of packets is not modified. In contrast to all previous passive timing based correlation approaches, our flow watermarking based correlation methods do not require the active timing perturbation introduced by the attacker to follow any particular distribution or random process to be effective.

4.2   Quantization Based Flow Watermarking

4.2.1   Watermarking Model and Concept

Traditional digital watermarking [13] consists of some watermark carrier, and two complementary processes: encoding and decoding. The watermark encoding process embeds the watermark information into the carrier signal by a slight distortion of certain property of the carrier signal. The watermark decoding process detects and recovers the watermark information (equivalently, determines the existence of a given watermark) from given carrier signal. To correlate encrypted traffic, we use the inter-packet timing as the watermark carrier.

Given any bidirectional connection, we can split it into two unidirectional packet flows and process each separately. Given an unidirectional flow of $n > 1$ packets, assume its ith packet P_i arrives at some network node and leaves (i.e., forwarded) from some network node (e.g., stepping stone, gateway). Let t_i and t_i' be the arrival time and the departure time of packet P_i, respectively. Assume without loss of generality that the normal processing and queuing delay added by the network node is a constant $c > 0$, and that the attacker added an extra delay $d_i \geq 0$ to packet P_i at the same network node, then we have $t_i' = t_i + c + d_i$.

---

[1]We will address packet drop or bogus packets in later chapters.

We define the *arrival inter-packet delay* (AIPD) between P_i and P_j as

$$ipd_{i,j} = t_j - t_i \qquad (4.1)$$

and the *departure inter-packet delay* (DIPD) between P_i and P_j as

$$ipd'_{i,j} = t'_j - t'_i \qquad (4.2)$$

In the rest of the paper, when it is clear in the context, we will use IPD to denote either AIPD or DIPD. We further define the difference between $ipd'_{i,j}$ and $ipd_{i,j}$: $ipd'_{i,j} - ipd_{i,j} = d_j - d_i$ to be the adversary's *impact* or *perturbation* on $ipd_{i,j}$. In case some packets have been reordered during the transmission, we still the time stamp of the ith and the jth received packets (which may not correspond to the ith and the jth sent packets) to calculate $ipd_{i,j}$ or $ipd'_{i,j}$. Since only the time stamp of selected packets are used, the negative impact of using the "wrong" packets due to packet reorder is equivalent to some random timing perturbation over the IPD.

Let $D > 0$ be the maximum delay that the adversary can add to P_i ($i = 1, \ldots, n$), then range $[-D, D]$ is the *perturbation range* of the adversary such that its impact or perturbation $d_j - d_i \in [-D, D]$.

Given a flow of $n > 0$ packets: $P_1, \ldots, P_n$ with time stamps $t_1, \ldots, t_n$ respectively ($t_i < t_j$ for $1 \leq i < j \leq n$), we can independently and probabilistically choose $2m < n$ packets by the following process: (1) sequentially scan each of the n packets; and (2) independently and randomly determine if the current packet will be chosen for flow watermarking, with probability $p = \frac{2m}{n}$ ($0 < m < \frac{n}{2}$). In this process, the selection of one packet for flow watermarking is independent from the selection of any other packet(s). Therefore, we can expect to have $2m$ distinct packets independently and randomly selected from a packet flow of n packets.

4.2.2   Basic Watermark Bit Encoding and Decoding

Before we can encode any watermark bit into the IPD, we will first quantize the continuous value of IPD with some uniform quantization step size $s > 0$. Given any IPD $ipd > 0$, we define the *quantization of ipd* with uniform quantization step size $s > 0$ as the function

$$q(ipd, s) = round(ipd/s) \qquad (4.3)$$

where round(x) is the function that rounds off real number x to its nearest integer (i.e. round(x) = i for any $x \in [i - 0.5, \ i + 0.5)$).

Figure 4.2 illustrates the quantization of real value x. It is easy to see that $q(k \times s, s) = q(k \times s + y, s)$ for any integer k and any $y \in [-\frac{s}{2}, \frac{s}{2})$. The quantization essentially maps a given real value into an integer. Since IPD is non-negative in reality, the quantization of any IPD will be a non-negative integer.

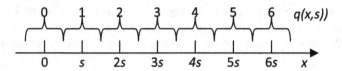

Fig. 4.2 Quantization of real value x

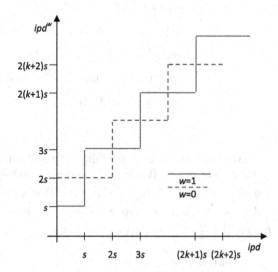

Fig. 4.3 Mapping between unwatermarked *ipd* and watermarked ipd^w to embed watermark bit w

Now we can encode the binary bit into the quantization of a given IPD. Let *ipd* be the original IPD before watermark bit w is encoded, and ipd^w be the IPD after watermark bit w is encode. To encode a binary bit w into an IPD, we slightly adjust that IPD such that the quantization of the adjusted IPD will have w as the modulo 2 remainder.

Given any $ipd > 0, s > 0$ and binary bit w, the watermark bit encoding function is defined as:

$$e(ipd, w, s) = [q(ipd + \frac{s}{2}, s) + \Delta] \times s \qquad (4.4)$$

where $\Delta = (w - (q(ipd + \frac{s}{2}, s) \mod 2) + 2) \mod 2$.

The encoding of one watermark bit w into scalar *ipd* is achieved by increasing the quantization of $ipd + \frac{s}{2}$ by the normalized difference between w and modulo 2 of the quantization of $ipd + \frac{s}{2}$. This ensures that the quantization of resulting ipd^w will have w as the remainder when modulus 2 operation is taken. The reason to quantize $ipd + \frac{s}{2}$ rather than *ipd* here is to make sure that the resulting $e(ipd, w, s)$ is no less than *ipd*. Figure 4.3 illustrates the encoding of watermark bit w by mapping ranges of unwatermarked *ipd* to the corresponding watermarked ipd^w.

The watermark bit decoding function is defined as

$$d(ipd^w, s) = q(ipd^w, s) \mod 2 \qquad (4.5)$$

Given any $ipd > 0$, we can find unique $a > 0$ and $-\frac{s}{2} < b \leq \frac{s}{2}$ such that $ipd + \frac{s}{2} = a \times s + b$. Then we have $q((ipd + \frac{s}{2}), s) = a$ and $e(ipd, w, s) = [a + ((w-a)$ mod $2 + 2)$ mod $2] \times s$. Therefore, for any $ipd > 0, s > 0$ and binary bit w,

$$d(e(ipd, w, s), s) \tag{4.6}$$

$$= q(e(ipd, w, s), s) \mod 2$$

$$= q([a + ((w-a) \mod 2 + 2) \mod 2] \times s) \mod 2$$

$$= \text{round}(a + ((w-a) \mod 2 + 2) \mod 2) \mod 2$$

$$= (a + ((w-a) \mod 2 + 2) \mod 2) \mod 2$$

$$= (a + w - a + 2) \mod 2$$

$$= w$$

This proves the correctness of the watermark encoding and decoding.

Given any $ipd > 0 ands > 0$, assume $\text{round}(\frac{ipd}{s} + \frac{1}{2}) = i$, by definition of round$(x)$, we have $\frac{ipd}{s} + \frac{1}{2} \in (\frac{i-1}{2}, \frac{i+1}{2}]$. That is $i - 1 < \frac{ipd}{s} \leq i$ or $(i - 1) \times s < ipd \leq i \times s$. Replace i with $\text{round}(\frac{ipd}{s} + \frac{1}{2})$, we have $\text{round}(\frac{ipd}{s} + \frac{1}{2}) \times s - s < ipd \leq \text{round}(\frac{ipd}{s} + \frac{1}{2}) \times s$. By Eq. (4.4), we have

$$d(e(ipd, w, s), s) \tag{4.7}$$

$$= [q((ipd + \frac{s}{2}), s) + (w - (q((ipd + \frac{s}{2}), s) \mod 2) + 2) \mod 2] \times s$$

$$\geq q((ipd + \frac{s}{2}), s) \times s$$

$$= \text{round}(\frac{ipd}{s} + \frac{1}{2}) \times s$$

$$\geq ipd$$

and

$$d(e(ipd, w, s), s) \tag{4.8}$$

$$= [q((ipd + \frac{s}{2}), s) + (w - (q((ipd + \frac{s}{2}), s) \mod 2) + 2) \mod 2] \times s$$

$$\leq [q((ipd + \frac{s}{2}), s) + 1] \times s$$

$$= \text{round}(\frac{ipd}{s} + \frac{1}{2}) \times s + s$$

$$\leq ipd + 2s$$

Therefore, $0 \leq e(ipd, w, s) - ipd < 2s$.

4.2.3 Maximum Tolerable Perturbation

Given any $ipd > 0, s > 0$, if we perturb ipd into $ipd \pm x$ $(x > 0)$, $d(ipd \pm x, s)$ remains the same as $d(ipd, s)$ until x reaches certain threshold. We call such a threshold the *maximum tolerable perturbation* Δ_{max} of $d(ipd, s)$. Specifically, either $d(ipd + \Delta_{max}, s) \neq d(ipd, s)$ or $d(ipd - \Delta_{max}, s) \neq d(ipd, s)$. And for all $0 < x < \Delta_{max}$, $d(ipd \pm x, s) = d(ipd, s)$ In other words, any smaller than Δ_{max} perturbation applied to ipd will not change the result of the watermark decoding, and a perturbation of Δ_{max} or greater may change the watermark decoding result.

The maximum tolerable perturbation partitions the perturbation range $[-D, D]$ into two parts: the *tolerable perturbation range* and the *vulnerable perturbation range*. The tolerable perturbation range is the portion of the perturbation range $[-D, D]$ within which any perturbation on ipd is guaranteed not to change $d(ipd, s)$, and the vulnerable perturbation range is range outside the tolerable perturbation range.

Given any $ipd > 0, s > 0$ and watermark bit w, from the quantization function $q(ipd, s)$ definition in (4.3) and watermark decoding function $d(ipd^w, s)$ definition in (4.5), it is easy to see that when $x \in [-\frac{s}{2}, \frac{s}{2})$, we have $d(e(ipd, w, s) + x, s) = d(e(ipd, w, s), s)$ and $d(e(ipd, w, s) + \frac{s}{2}, s) \neq d(e(ipd, w, s), s)$. Therefore, the maximum tolerable perturbation, the tolerable perturbation range and the vulnerable perturbation range of $d(ipd, s)$ are $\frac{s}{2}$, $[-\frac{s}{2}, \frac{s}{2})$ and $(-D, -\frac{s}{2}) \cup [\frac{s}{2}, D)$, respectively.

In summary, when the timing perturbation is within the tolerable perturbation range $[-\frac{s}{2}, \frac{s}{2})$, it is guaranteed not corrupt the encoded watermark. Therefore, bigger quantization step s will give us better resistance to timing perturbations. However, watermark encoding with bigger quantization step s will result larger distortion as the watermark encoding itself may introduce up to $2s$ delay to selected packets.

It is desirable to have a watermark encoding scheme that (1) has little watermark encoding distortion to the inter-packet timing, so that the watermark encoding is stealthier; and (2) is robust, with high probability, against timing perturbations larger than the maximum tolerable perturbation $\frac{s}{2}$.

In next section, we address the case when the maximum timing perturbation D introduced by the adversary is larger than the maximum tolerable perturbation $\frac{s}{2}$. While we can never eliminate the probability that a timing perturbation larger than $\frac{s}{2}$ could corrupt the encoded watermark bit, we want to minimize such probability and make the encoded watermark bit probabilistically robust against large random timing perturbations by the adversary. By utilizing redundancy techniques, we could indeed make the encoded watermark bit robust against arbitrarily large (and yet bounded) random timing perturbation by the adversary, as long as the flow to be watermarked contains is long enough and has enough of packets.

4.2.4   Encoding a Single Watermark Bit Over the Average of Multiple IPDs

The key to make the encoded watermark bit probabilistically robust against timing perturbation larger than $\frac{s}{2}$ is to contain and minimize the impact of the timing perturbation such that the impact of the timing perturbation will fall, with high probability, within the tolerable perturbation range $[-\frac{s}{2}, \frac{s}{2})$. We use two strategies to achieve this goal. First, we spread the watermark-bearing IPDs over a longer duration of the packet flow. Second, we encode a watermark bit in the *average* of multiple IPDs that are distributed over a long duration of the packet flow. These strategies essentially exploit the assumption that the adversary does not know exactly which packets are randomly selected and which IPDs between those randomly selected packets will be used for encoding the watermark.

While the adversary may introduce a large impact to any single IPD, it is infeasible for him to introduce the same impact to all the randomly chosen IPDs. In fact, random delays tend to increase some IPDs and decrease others. Due to the self-canceling effect, the impact on the average of multiple IPDs tend to be within the tolerable perturbation range $[-\frac{s}{2}, \frac{s}{2})$, even when the perturbation range $[-D, D]$ is much larger than $[-\frac{s}{2}, \frac{s}{2})$. Based on this observation, we encode the watermark bit into the average of $m \geq 1$ randomly chosen IPDs, where m is the *redundancy number*.

Given a packet flow of $n > 1$ packets: $P_1, \ldots, P_n$ with corresponding time stamps $t_1, \ldots, t_n$ ($t_i < t_j$ for $1 \leq i < j \leq n$), we first independently and randomly choose $2m$ ($0 < m < \frac{n}{2}$) distinct packets: $P_{x_1}, \ldots, P_{x_{2m}}$ ($1 \leq x_k \leq n$ for $1 \leq k \leq 2m$). We then independently and randomly pick two distinct packets from those $2m$ packets. Let P_{y_1} be the packet with smaller time stamp, and P_{z_1} be the packet with bigger time stamp. Repeating the above independent process enough times, we can expect to obtain m distinct packet pairs: $\{< P_{y_1}, P_{z_1} >, \ldots, < P_{y_m}, P_{z_m} >\}$ ($y_k < z_k$ and $y_k, z_k \in \{x_1, \ldots, x_{2m}\}$). Then we have m IPDs: $ipd_k = t_{z_k} - t_{y_k} (k = 1, \ldots, m)$. We represent the average of these m IPDs as

$$ipd_{avg} = \frac{1}{m} \sum_{k=1}^{m} ipd_k \qquad (4.9)$$

Given any $ipd_{avg} > 0$, quantization step $s > 0$ and the watermark bit to be encoded w, we can encode w into ipd_{avg} by applying the encoding function defined in Eq. (4.4) to ipd_{avg}. Specifically, we can add even delay Δ to packets P_{z_k} ($k = 1, \ldots, m$) so that ipd_{avg} is adjusted by Δ, as defined in Eq. (4.4). To decode the watermark bit, we first obtain the m IPDs (denoted as $ipd_k^w, k = 1, \ldots, m$) from the same m pairs of randomly selected packets and the average ipd_{avg}^w of $ipd_1^w, \ldots, ipd_m^w$. Then we can apply the decoding function defined in Eq. (4.5) to ipd_{avg}^w to obtain the watermark bit.

When adjusting the average of those m IPDs, it is desirable to delay each of the watermark bearing IPDs evenly. This, however, requires the watermark encoding process to know the exact values of those IPDs to be averaged before deciding how what the even delay is. In real-time communication, incoming packets arrive one by one, and the watermark encoding process can not buffer those incoming packets for too long before forwarding them. Therefore, the watermark encoding process may need to adjust the timing of some packets and send them out before receiving all those watermark-bearing packets in the m selected IPDs. In this case, the watermark encoding process may add uneven delay to those watermark-bearing packets.

4.2.5 Analysis of Watermark Decoding in the Presence of Timing Perturbations

Based on very moderate assumptions about the active timing perturbations, we establish an upper bound as well as an approximation to the watermark bit decoding error probability in the presence of active timing perturbation.

4.2.5.1 Upper Bound of the Watermark Bit Decoding Error Probability

Let D_i ($i = 1, \ldots, n$) be the random delays the adversary adds to packets P_i ($i = 1, \ldots, n$), and $D > 0$ be the maximum delay the adversary can add to any packet. Here we do not require the random delays D_i to follow any particular distribution, except that the random delays D_i follow some distribution of finite variance. For example, distribution of D_i may be deterministic, bimodal, self-similar, or any other distribution. Furthermore, we do not require the random delay D_is to be independent from each other, and we only assume that the covariance between different D_i's is fixed.

Since the adversary does not know which packets are randomly selected by the watermark encoder, and the selection of watermark encoding packet P_{x_k} ($k = 1, \ldots, 2m$) is independent from any random delays D_i the adversary may add, the impact of the adversary's delays over randomly selected P_{x_k}'s is equivalent to randomly choosing one from the random variable list $D_1, \ldots, D_n$. Let d_k ($k = 1, \ldots, 2m$) be the random variable representing the impact of the adversary's random delays over the kth randomly selected packet P_{x_k}. Then d_k's ($k = 1, \ldots, 2m$) are identically distributed as the adversary's random delays follow some fixed distribution.

Let d_{y_k} and d_{z_k} be the random variables that represent the adversary's random delays to packets P_{y_k} and P_{z_k} respectively for $k = 1, \ldots, m$. Then random variable $X_k = d_{z_k} - d_{y_k}$ represents the overall impact of these random delays on $ipd_k = t_{z_k} - t_{y_k}$, and we have $E(X_k) = 0$. We use random variable $\overline{X_m}$ to denote the overall impact of random delay on ipd_{avg}. From Eq. (4.9), we have

$$\overline{X_m} = \frac{1}{m}\sum_{k=1}^{m}(d_{z_k} - d_{y_k}) = \frac{1}{m}\sum_{k=1}^{m}X_k \tag{4.10}$$

Therefore the overall impact of the adversary's random delay over ipd_{avg} is essentially the sample mean of $X_1, \ldots, X_m$. For the watermark bit encoded in the average of multiple IPDs, the watermark bit vulnerability $\Pr(|\overline{X_m}| \geq \frac{s}{2})$ is the probability that the impact of the adversary's timing perturbation is out of the tolerable perturbation range $(-\frac{s}{2}, \frac{s}{2}]$, which may corrupt the encoded watermark bit.

Let μ and σ^2 be the mean and the variance of the adversary's random delay. Because the adversary's random delay is bounded, σ^2 is finite. Given $\text{Cov}(u, v) = E(uv) - E(u)E(v)$, $E(d_{z_i}) = E(d_{z_j}) = E(d_{y_i}) = E(d_{y_j})$ and $\text{Cov}(D_i, D_j)$ $(i \neq j)$ is constant, we have

$$E(d_{z_i}d_{z_j}) = E(d_{y_i}d_{y_j}) = E(d_{z_i}d_{y_j}) = E(d_{z_j}d_{y_i}) \tag{4.11}$$

Then

$$\text{Cov}(X_i, X_j) = E(X_iX_j) \tag{4.12}$$
$$= E((d_{z_i} - d_{y_i})(d_{z_j} - d_{y_j}))$$
$$= E(d_{z_i}d_{z_j}) + E(d_{y_i}d_{y_j}) - E(d_{z_i}d_{y_j}) - E(d_{z_j}d_{y_i})$$
$$= 0$$

Therefore

$$\text{Var}(\overline{X_m}) = \frac{1}{m^2}\text{Var}(\sum_{k=1}^{m}X_k) \tag{4.13}$$

$$= \frac{1}{m^2}[\sum_{k=1}^{m}\text{Var}(X_k) + 2\text{Cov}(X_i, X_j)]_{1 \leq i < j \leq m}$$

$$= \frac{1}{m}\text{Var}(X_k)$$

$$\leq \frac{4\sigma^2}{m}$$

According to the Chebyshev inequality in statistics [16], given any random variable X with finite variance $\text{Var}(X)$ and any $t > 0$, $\Pr(|X - E(X)| \geq t) \leq \text{Var}(X)/t^2$. Applying the Chebyshev inequality to $\overline{X_m}$ with $t = \frac{s}{2}$, we have

$$\Pr(|\overline{X_m}| \geq \frac{s}{2}) \leq \frac{16\sigma^2}{ms^2} \tag{4.14}$$

Since the watermark bit decoding could be correct even when the overall impact of the adversary's random delay is outside the tolerable perturbation range, the actual watermark bit decoding error probability is less than $\Pr(|\overline{X_m}| \geq \frac{s}{2})$. Therefore, above inequality essentially establishes an upper bound of watermark bit decoding error probability.

The important result here is that given arbitrarily small quantization step $s > 0$ and arbitrarily large (but bounded) σ^2, we can always make the upper bound $\frac{16\sigma^2}{ms^2}$ arbitrarily close to 0 by having large enough redundancy number m. This result holds true regardless of the distribution, mean or the variance of the adversary's random delays. Furthermore, the upper bound of the watermark bit decoding error probability holds true even if the random delays on different packets are correlated provided the covariance is fixed.

4.2.5.2 Approximation to the Watermark Bit Robustness

In this subsection, we derive an accurate approximation to the watermark bit robustness $\Pr(|\overline{X_m}| < \frac{s}{2})$ assuming the adversary's random delays are independent and identically distributed (*iid*). Our empirical evaluation demonstrates that the approximation model works well for non-*iid* (e.g. batch-releasing) random delays.

Central Limit Theorem. *If the random variables $X_1, \ldots, X_n$ form a random sample of size n from a given distribution X with mean μ and finite variance σ^2, then for any fixed number x*

$$\lim_{n \to \infty} \Pr[\frac{\sqrt{n}(\overline{X_n} - \mu)}{\sigma} \leq x] = \Phi(x) \tag{4.15}$$

where $\Phi(x) = \int_{-\infty}^{x} \frac{1}{\sqrt{2\pi}} e^{-\frac{u^2}{2}} du$.

The theorem essentially states that whenever a random sample of size n is taken from any distribution with mean μ and finite variance σ^2, the sample mean $\overline{X_n}$ will be approximately normally distributed with mean μ and variance σ^2/n, or equivalently the distribution of random variable $\sqrt{n}(\overline{X_n} - \mu)/\sigma$ will be approximately a standard normal distribution.

Let σ^2 be the variance of the distribution of the adversary's random delays (i.e., let $\mathrm{Var}(d_{y_k}) = \mathrm{Var}(d_{z_k}) = \sigma^2$). Apply the Central Limit Theorem to random sample $X_1 = d_{z_1} - d_{y_1}, \ldots, X_m = d_{z_m} - d_{y_m}$, where $\mathrm{Var}(X_k) = \mathrm{Var}(d_{z_k}) + \mathrm{Var}(d_{y_k}) = 2\sigma^2$ and $E(X_k) = E(d_{z_k}) - E(d_{y_k}) = 0$, we have

$$\Pr[\frac{\sqrt{m}(\overline{X_m} - E(X_i))}{\sqrt{\mathrm{Var}(X_i)}} < x] = \Pr[\frac{\sqrt{m}\overline{X_m}}{\sqrt{2}\sigma} < x] \approx \Phi(x) \tag{4.16}$$

Since $\Phi(x)$ is symmetric, we have

$$\Pr[|\frac{\sqrt{m}\overline{X}_m}{\sqrt{2}\sigma}| < x] \approx 2\Phi(x) - 1 \qquad (4.17)$$

We further have

$$p = \Pr[|\overline{X}_m| < \frac{s}{2}] = \Pr[|\frac{\sqrt{m}\overline{X}_m}{\sqrt{2}\sigma}| < \frac{s\sqrt{m}}{2\sqrt{2}\sigma}] \approx 2\Phi(\frac{s\sqrt{m}}{2\sqrt{2}\sigma}) - 1 \qquad (4.18)$$

Therefore, the impact of the adversary's timing perturbation on the encoded watermark bit is approximately normally distributed with zero mean and variance $2\sigma^2/m$. Although the encoded watermark bit could be decoded correctly even if the adversary's timing perturbation falls outside $(-\frac{s}{2}, \frac{s}{2})$, such a probability is very small when p is close to 1. Therefore, p is a conservative approximation to the probability that the encoded watermark bit will survive the adversary's timing perturbation.

Equation (4.18) is consistent with the result of (4.14). Figure 4.4 illustrates how the distribution of the impact of the adversary's random timing perturbations can be "squeezed" more into the tolerable perturbation range by increasing the number of IPDs averaged.

Equation (4.18) enables us to estimate the watermark bit robustness accurately. For example, assume the adversary's maximum delay is normalized to 1 time unit, the adversary's random delays are uniformly distributed over $[0, 1]$ (whose variance σ^2 is 1/12), $s = 0.4$, and $m = 12$, then $\Pr[|\overline{X}_{12}| < 0.2] \approx 2\Phi(1.2 \times \sqrt{2}) - 1 \approx 91\%$. In other words, although the random delay is uniformly distributed in range $[0, 1]$ whose timing perturbation range is $[-1, 1]$, the impact of random timing perturbations on the average of 12 IPDs will fall within the range $[-0.2, 0.2]$ with about 91 % probability. Table 4.1 shows the

Fig. 4.4 Impact of random timing perturbations, for different values of the redundancy number m

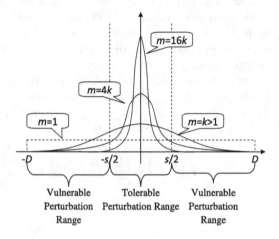

Table 4.1 Watermark bit robustness simulation for uniformly distributed random delays over [0, 1], $s = 0.4$

m	7	8	9	10	11	12
Estimated robustness (%)	80.46	83.32	85.54	87.86	89.58	91.02
Simulated robustness (%)	80.27	83.27	85.68	87.79	89.54	91.02

estimation and simulation measurement of watermark bit robustness with uniformly distributed random delays over [0, 1], $s = 0.4$ and various values of the redundancy number m. This demonstrates that the Central Limit Theorem could give us a very accurate estimate for a sample size as small as $m = 7$.

Equation (4.18) also shows that it is easier to achieve a desired level of robustness by increasing s than by increasing m. For example, increasing s by a factor of 2 has the same effect as increasing m by a factor of 4.

4.2.5.3 Analysis of Watermark Detectability and Collision

Given a packet flow f, watermark detection determines if f has the specified watermark encoded. Let $< S, m, l, s, w >$ be the secret information shared between the watermark encoder and decoder, where S is the packet selection function that returns $2ml$ packets, $m \geq 1$ is the number of redundant pairs of packets for encoding one watermark bit, $l > 0$ is the length of the watermark in bits, $s > 0$ is the quantization step, and w is the l-bit watermark to be detected. Let w_f the l bits decoded from flow f.

The watermark detector has the following steps:

1. Decode the l-bit w_f from flow f.
2. Compare the decoded w_f with w and calculate $H(w_f, w)$: the Hamming distance between w_f and w.
3. If $H(w_f, w) \leq h$ (h is a configurable threshold and $0 \leq h < l$), then report detection of watermark w from flow f; Otherwise, report watermark w not detected from flow f.

Instead of requiring the exact match of all the watermark bits w, we use the Hamming distance to allow up to h bits mismatch. Such relaxed match helps to increase the detection rate of the watermark detector i the presence of active timing perturbations by the adversary. Given any quantization step size $s > 0$, when the adversary's maximum delay is bigger than s, there is always a non-zero probability that the adversary's timing perturbation could corrupt the encoded watermark bits, no matter how much redundancy is used. Let $0 < p < 1$ be the probability that each encoded watermark bit will survive the adversary's timing perturbation. Then the probability that all l bits survive the adversary's timing perturbation p^l. When l is reasonably large, p^l tends to be small unless p is very close to 1. Therefore, the expected watermark detection rate with the exact match of all the watermark bits will be quite low.

On the other hand, the expected watermark detection rate with Hamming distance h will be

$$\text{TPR}(l, h, p) = \sum_{i=0}^{h} \binom{l}{i} p^{l-i} (1-p)^i \tag{4.19}$$

This will substantially increase the expected watermark detection rate. For example, for the value $p = 0.9102, l = 24$, the expected watermark detection rate with exact match would be $p^l = 10.45\%$. The expected watermark detection rate with Hamming distance $h = 5$ would be 98.29 %.

Given an unwatermarked packet flow f, and a l-bit watermark w and a Hamming distance threshold $h > 0$, there is a slight chance that the unwatermarked flow f happens to have at least $l-h$ bits of w matched. In this case, $H(w_f, w) \le h$ (w_f is the l-bit decoding from the unwatermarked flow f), and the watermark detector would report watermark w detected from the unwatermarked flow f. We term this situation as a *collision* between w and f with Hamming distance h.

Assuming the l-bit w_f decoded from a random flow f is uniformly distributed, then the expected watermark collision probability between any particular watermark w and a random flow f will be

$$\text{FPR}(l, h) = \sum_{i=0}^{h} \binom{l}{i} (\frac{1}{2})^l \tag{4.20}$$

Figure 4.5 illustrates the derived probability distribution of the expected watermark detection rate and the expected watermark collision rate for $l = 24$ and $p = 0.9102$. Given any number of watermark bits $l > 1$ and any watermark bit robustness $0 < p < 1$, the bigger the Hamming distance threshold h is, the higher the expected watermarked detection rate will be. However, a bigger Hamming distance threshold

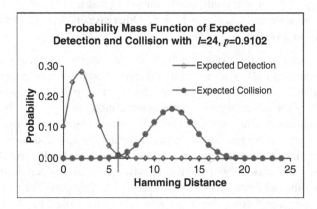

Fig. 4.5 Effect of the threshold h on the detection and collision rates of the watermarking method

tends to increase the expected watermark detection collision (false positive) rate of at the same time. An optimal Hamming distance threshold h would give both high expected watermark detection rate and low expected watermark detection false positive rate at the same time. The optimal h and l depend on (1) the number of packets available; (2) the defining characteristics of the active timing perturbation; and (3) how to measure the combined watermarked detection rate and collision rate. Before we analyze the optimality, we show that our flow watermarking scheme can be effective even with potentially suboptimal h and l.

Given any quantization step $s > 0$, any desired watermark collision probability $0 < P_c < 1$, and any desired watermark detection rate $0 < P_d < 1$, we can always find appropriate watermark length $l > 0$ and Hamming distance threshold $0 \leq h < l$ to meet both the watermark collision and detection requirements at the same time. We first choose some Hamming distance threshold $0 \leq h < \frac{l}{2}$, then we have

$$\sum_{i=0}^{h} \binom{l}{i}(\frac{1}{2})^l \leq \sum_{i=0}^{h} \binom{l}{h}(\frac{1}{2})^l \leq (h+1)\frac{l^h}{2^l} \qquad (4.21)$$

Since $\lim_{l \to \infty} \frac{l^h}{2^l} = 0$, we can always make the expected watermark collision probability $\mathrm{FPR}(l, h) < P_c$ by having sufficiently large watermark bit number l. Because $\sum_{i=0}^{h} \binom{l}{i} p^{l-i}(1-p)^i \geq p^l$, we can always make the expected detection rate $\mathrm{TPR}(l, h, p) > P_d$ by making p sufficiently close to 1. From inequality (4.14), this can be achieved by having sufficiently large redundancy number m given any fixed values of s and σ.

In theory, the quantization based flow watermarking scheme can achieve, arbitrarily close to 100 % watermark detection rate and arbitrarily close to 0 % watermark collision probability at the same time against arbitrarily large (but bounded) random timing perturbation of arbitrary distribution with arbitrarily small averaged adjustment of inter-packet timing, as long as the flow to be watermarked is long enough and has enough packets.

Theoretically, there exist some special case such that large enough timing perturbation could potentially completely remove the encoded watermark. For example, with sufficiently large delay, the inter-packet timing of the watermarked packet flow could be perturbed into some constant (i.e., the IPDs between all adjacent packets equal to the average IPDs). In this case, the watermark decoding of the constant-rated flow would be fixed. However, achieving such a complete elimination of the encoded watermark requires knowledge of the exact timing characteristics of the whole duration of the packet flow, which is normally not available in real-time communication. We will further analyze the fundamental limitation of the adversary's timing perturbations under the constraints of real-time communication in Sect. 6.4.

In practice, the number of packets in the packet flow is a fundamental limiting factor to the achievable effectiveness of the quantization based flow watermarking scheme. Our experiences demonstrate that quantization based flow watermarking can be effective on flows with as few as several hundred packets. Specifically, our experiments show that quantization based flow watermarking can achieve a virtually 100 % watermark decoding rate against up to 1000 ms random timing perturbation, and less than 0.35 % false positive rate at the same time with less than 300 packets.

4.2.6   Optimality Analysis

4.2.6.1   Embedding Watermark in Binary Form vs. Non-binary Form

We have presented how to embed the watermark digits into the IPDs in binary form. However, the watermark digits can actually be embedded in non-binary form. In this subsection, we prove that embedding the watermark digits in binary form is optimal in term of number of packets needed.

Assume the maximum allowed averaged timing adjustment is $C > 0$, the maximum quantization steps for embedding watermark digits in binary form and non-binary form (with based $b > 2$) are s_2 and s_b respectively. Then we have $2 \times s_2 = b \times s_b = C$. That is $s_b = \frac{2s_2}{b}$.

Assume the entropy (number of binary bits) of the watermark information needs to be embedded is l_2. Let l_b denote the minimum number of non-binary digits (of base $b > 2$) needed to represent l_2 binary digits. We have $l_b = \log_b 2 \times l_2$.

Let m_2 and m_b denote the redundancy numbers needed to achieve the same watermark bit robustness in binary form and non-binary form of base b respectively. From Eq. (4.18), we have $s_2 \sqrt{m_2} = s_b \sqrt{m_b}$. Replace s_b with $\frac{2s_2}{b}$, we get $m_b = b^2 \times \frac{m_2}{4}$.

Therefore, the number of IPDs needed to embed l_b digits of base b is

$$l_b \times m_b = (\log_b 2 \times l_2) \times (\frac{b^2 \times m_2}{4}) = \frac{b^2}{4 \log_2 b} \times l_2 m_2$$

It is easy to see that $\frac{b^2}{4 \log_2 b} > 1$ for $b > 2$. That means it takes more IPDs to embed same amount of information in non-binary form than in binary form.

In summary, given any particular maximum timing adjustment allowed for embedding watermark of certain amount of information, it is optimal to embed watermark in binary form, which requires less packets to be adjusted than any non-binary form.

4.2.6.2   Optimal Hamming Distance Threshold

Equations (4.19) and (4.20) give the expected watermark detection true positive rate (TPR) and false positive rate (FPR) respectively.

The expected watermark detection false negative rate (FNR = 1-TPR) can be thought as a function of l, h and p:

$$\text{FNR}(l, h, p) = 1 - \sum_{i=0}^{h} \binom{l}{i} p^{l-i}(1-p)^i \qquad (4.22)$$

Given the number of watermark bits $l > 0$, the probability of recovering the embedded watermark bit (in the presence of timing perturbation) $\frac{1}{2} < p < 1$, increasing Hamming distance threshold h will increase FPR(l, h) and decrease FNR(l, h, p) at the same time, and decreasing h will decrease FPR(l, h) and increase FNR(l, h, p) at the same time. Given any particular $l > 0$ and $0.5 < p < 1$ we want to determine the optimal Hamming distance threshold h that will give minimum combined watermark detection false positive rate and false negative rate:

$$f(l, h, p) = \text{FPR}(l, h) + \text{FNR}(l, h, p) \qquad (4.23)$$

$$= \sum_{i=0}^{h} \binom{l}{i}(\tfrac{1}{2})^l + 1 - \sum_{i=0}^{h} \binom{l}{i} p^{l-i}(1-p)^i$$

Because $\frac{1}{2} < p < 1$, the mode of binomial distribution $\binom{l}{i} p^{l-i}(1-p)^i$ must be less than the mode of binomial distribution $\binom{l}{i}(\tfrac{1}{2})^l$. Then there must exist unique real value $h_x \in [(l+1)(1-p) - 1, \frac{l+1}{2}]$ such that

$$p^{l-h_x}(1-p)^{h_x} = (\tfrac{1}{2})^l \qquad (4.24)$$

In addition, $p^{l-\lfloor h_x \rfloor}(1-p)^{\lfloor h_x \rfloor} \le (\tfrac{1}{2})^l$ and $p^{l-\lceil h_x \rceil}(1-p)^{\lceil h_x \rceil} \ge (\tfrac{1}{2})^l$.

In Fig. 4.5 where $l = 24, p = 0.9102$, the mode of $\binom{l}{i} p^{l-i}(1-p)^i$ is 2 and the mode of $\binom{l}{i}(\tfrac{1}{2})^l$ is 12. $p^{l-h_x}(1-p)^{h_x} = (\tfrac{1}{2})^l$ only when $h_x \approx 6$. For any $h > \lceil h_x \rceil$, $p^{l-h}(1-p)^h < (\tfrac{1}{2})^l$, for any $h < \lfloor h_x \rfloor$, $p^{l-h}(1-p)^h > (\tfrac{1}{2})^l$.

Because $\frac{1}{2} < p < 1$, for any $i > 0$, $(\frac{p}{1-p})^i > 1$ and $(\frac{1-p}{p})^i < 1$. Therefore, we have

$$p^{l-\lfloor h_x \rfloor}(1-p)^{\lfloor h_x \rfloor}(\frac{p}{1-p})^i - (\tfrac{1}{2})^l > p^{l-\lfloor h_x \rfloor}(1-p)^{\lfloor h_x \rfloor} - (\tfrac{1}{2})^l \ge 0$$

and

$$(\tfrac{1}{2})^l - p^{l-\lceil h_x \rceil}(1-p)^{\lceil h_x \rceil}(\frac{1-p}{p})^i > (\tfrac{1}{2})^l - p^{l-\lceil h_x \rceil}(1-p)^{\lceil h_x \rceil} \ge 0$$

If we choose to use $\lfloor h_x \rfloor$ as the Hamming distance threshold, then the combined FPR and FNR with any smaller Hamming distance threshold $\lfloor h_x \rfloor - k$ $(k \geq 1)$ is

$$f(l, \lfloor h_x \rfloor - k, p) = f(l, \lfloor h_x \rfloor, p) + \sum_{i=0}^{k-1} \binom{l}{\lfloor h_x \rfloor - i} [p^{l - \lfloor h_x \rfloor + i}(1 - p)^{\lfloor h_x \rfloor - i} - (\frac{1}{2})^l]$$

$$= f(l, \lfloor h_x \rfloor, p) + \sum_{i=0}^{k-1} \binom{l}{\lfloor h_x \rfloor - i} [p^{l - \lfloor h_x \rfloor}(1 - p)^{\lfloor h_x \rfloor}(\frac{p}{1-p})^i - (\frac{1}{2})^l]$$

$$> f(l, \lfloor h_x \rfloor, p) \tag{4.25}$$

If we choose to use $\lceil h_x \rceil$ as the Hamming distance threshold, then the combined FPR and FNR with any bigger Hamming distance threshold $\lceil h_x \rceil + k$ $(k \geq 1)$ is

$$f(l, \lceil h_x \rceil + k, p) = f(l, \lceil h_x \rceil, p) + \sum_{i=1}^{k} \binom{l}{\lceil h_x \rceil + i} [(\frac{1}{2})^l - p^{l - \lceil h_x \rceil - i}(1 - p)^{\lceil h_x \rceil + i}]$$

$$= f(l, \lceil h_x \rceil, p) + \sum_{i=1}^{k} \binom{l}{\lceil h_x \rceil + i} [(\frac{1}{2})^l - p^{l - \lceil h_x \rceil}(1 - p)^{\lceil h_x \rceil}(\frac{1-p}{p})^i]$$

$$> f(l, \lceil h_x \rceil, p) \tag{4.26}$$

Therefore, the optimal Hamming distance for achieving the minial combined watermark detection false positive rate and false negative rate $f(l, h, p)$ is either $\lfloor h_x \rfloor$ or $\lceil h_x \rceil$ where h_x satisfies Eq. (4.24).

Solving Eq. (4.24), we get

$$h_x = \frac{\log_2 p + 1}{\log_2 p - \log_2(1 - p)} l \tag{4.27}$$

Note, the optimal Hamming distance result holds true for not only the quantization based flow watermarking scheme, but also other flow watermarking methods that use binary form watermarks.

4.3 Probabilistic Flow Watermarking

To make the watermark encoding more stealthy, it is desirable to have even delay on those selected packets When encoding a given watermark into the inter-packet timing of a given flow. The quantization based flow watermarking scheme described in Sect. 4.2, however, usually has uneven delay on randomly selected packets when there is not enough buffering due to real-time constraints.

Now we present a probabilistic flow watermarking scheme that guarantees the even delay on selected packets when encoding any give watermark to a given packet flow in real time. By exploiting the inherent inter-packet timing characteristics of the packet flows, the probabilistic flow watermarking scheme requires fewer packets to achieve the same effectiveness and robustness of the quantization base flow watermarking scheme.

4.3.1 Basic Concept and Notion

Given a constant integer $d \geq 1$ and any packet flow of $n \gg d$ packets: $P_1, \ldots, P_n$ with corresponding time stamps $t_1, \ldots, t_n$ ($t_i < t_j$ for $1 \leq i < j \leq n$), we can independently and probabilistically choose $2r$ ($1 \leq r < \frac{n-d}{2}$) packets from the packet flow via the following process: (1) sequentially scan the first $n - d$ packets; and (2) independently choose the current packet with probability $p = \frac{2r}{n-d}$.

Then we can expect to have $2r$ distinct packets independently and randomly selected from the given packet flow of n packets. From the $2r$ randomly selected packets $P_{z_1}, \ldots, P_{z_{2r}}$ ($1 \leq z_k \leq n - d$ for $1 \leq k \leq 2r$), we can create $2r$ packet pairs: $\langle P_{z_k}, P_{z_k+d} \rangle$ ($d \geq 1$, $k = 1, \ldots, 2r$). Here r is the redundancy number.

We define the IPD (Inter-Packet Delay) between P_{z_k+d} and P_{z_k} as

$$ipd_{z_k,d} = t_{z_k+d} - t_{z_k}, \quad (k = 1, \ldots, 2r) \tag{4.28}$$

Assume the IPD of the packet flow follows some fixed distribution of finite variation, then $ipd_{z_k,d}$ is identically distributed. Because all P_{z_k} ($k = 1, \ldots, 2r$) are selected independently, $ipd_{z_k,d}$ is independent from each other. Therefore, $ipd_{z_k,d}$ ($k = 1, \ldots, 2r$) is independent and identically distributed (*iid*).

We randomly divide the $2r$ IPDs into 2 groups of equal size, and use $ipd_{1,k,d}$ and $ipd_{2,k,d}$ ($k = 1, \ldots, r$) to denote the r IPDs in group 1 and group 2 respectively. Given that all $ipd_{1,k,d}$ and $ipd_{2,k,d}$ ($k = 1, \ldots, r$) are *iid*, we have $E(ipd_{1,k,d}) = E(ipd_{2,k,d})$, and $Var(ipd_{1,k,d}) = Var(ipd_{2,k,d})$.

Let

$$Y_{k,d} = \frac{ipd_{1,k,d} - ipd_{2,k,d}}{2} \quad (k = 1, \ldots, r) \tag{4.29}$$

Then $ipd_{2,k,d}$ ($k = 1, \ldots, r$) is *iid*, and $E(Y_{k,d}) = 0$. We use $\sigma_{Y,d}^2$ to denote the variance of $Y_{k,d}$, and we represent the average of r $Y_{k,d}$'s as

$$\overline{Y_{r,d}} = \frac{1}{r} \sum_{k=1}^{r} Y_{k,d} \tag{4.30}$$

Then we have $E(\overline{Y_{r,d}}) = 0$. Given $Y_{k,d}$ is symmetric ($k = 1, \ldots, r$), $\overline{Y_{r,d}}$ is also symmetric. Since $Y_{k,d}$ is *iid*, we have $\text{Var}(\overline{Y_{r,d}}) = \frac{\sigma_{Y,d}^2}{r}$.

4.3.2 Encoding and Decoding a Binary Bit Probabilistically

Because the distribution of $\overline{Y_{r,d}}$ is symmetric and $E(\overline{Y_{r,d}}) = 0$, $\overline{Y_{r,d}}$ has equal probability to be positive and negative. To probabilistically encode a bit 0, we decrease $\overline{Y_{r,d}}$ by a so that it will be more likely to be less than 0. To probabilistically encode a bit 1, we increase $\overline{Y_{r,d}}$ by a so that it will have >0.5 probability to be greater than 0. Figure 4.6 illustrates such probabilistic encoding of a binary bit.

By definition in Eq. (4.30), decreasing or increasing each of the r $Y_{k,d}$'s by a would decrease or increase $\overline{Y_{r,d}}$ by a. By definition in Eq. (4.29), decreasing each $ipd_{1,k,d}$ by a and increasing each $ipd_{2,k,d}$ by a would decrease $Y_{k,d}$ by a, and increasing each $ipd_{1,k,d}$ by a and decreasing each $ipd_{2,k,d}$ by a would increase $Y_{k,d}$ by a.

To decode $\overline{Y_{r,d}}$, we simply check if it is great than 0 or not. If $\overline{Y_{r,d}} > 0$, then the decoding is 1; otherwise the decoding is 0. Once a bit has been encoded into $\overline{Y_{r,d}}$ (i.e., it has been decreased or increased by a), the probability to have correct decoding from $\overline{Y_{r,d}}$ is always greater than that of wrong decoding.

Due the symmetry of the distribution of $\overline{Y_{r,d}}$, $\text{Pr}(\overline{Y_{r,d}} < a)$ is the probability that the encoded bit will be decoded correctly. Here the timing adjustment a is essentially a representation of the signal strength of the encoded watermark bit. The larger the a is, the more likely the encoded watermark bit will be decoded correctly. We now show that we can achieve arbitrarily close to 100 % correct decoding probability with arbitrarily small $a > 0$ (or equivalently arbitrarily weak signal strength) by having a sufficiently large redundancy number r.

Applying the Central Limit Theorem to random sample $Y_{1,d}, \ldots, Y_{r,d}$, where $\text{Var}(Y_{k,d}) = \sigma_{Y,d}^2$, $E(Y_{k,d}) = 0$, we have

$$\text{Pr}[\frac{\sqrt{r}(\overline{Y_{r,d}} - E(Y_{k,d}))}{\sqrt{\text{Var}(Y_{r,d})}} < x] = \text{Pr}[\frac{\sqrt{r}\overline{Y_{r,d}}}{\sigma_{Y,d}} < x] \approx \Phi(x) \tag{4.31}$$

Fig. 4.6 Encoding binary bit by shifting the distribution of $\overline{Y_{r,d}}$ by a to the left or right

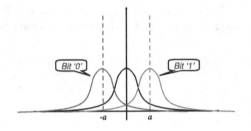

Fig. 4.7 Probability distribution of $\overline{Y_{r,d}}$ with different r

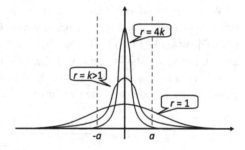

We further have

$$\Pr[\overline{Y_{r,d}} < a] = \Pr[\frac{\sqrt{r}\overline{Y_{r,d}}}{\sigma_{Y,d}} < \frac{a\sqrt{r}}{\sigma_{Y,d}}] \approx \Phi(\frac{a\sqrt{r}}{\sigma_{Y,d}}) \tag{4.32}$$

Equation (4.32) gives us an accurate estimate of the probability that an encoded watermark will be decoded correctly. The important result here is: no matter how small the timing adjustment $a > 0$ (i.e., the watermark encoding signal strength) might be, we can always make the probability of correct watermark bit decoding arbitrarily close to 100 % by simply increasing the redundancy number r. This result holds true regardless of the distribution of the inter-packet timing of the packet flow. Figure 4.7 illustrates how increasing the redundancy number r could "squeeze" the distribution of $\overline{Y_{r,d}}$ into range $[-a, a]$, which will guarantee correct watermark bit decoding.

Now we analyze the negative impact of timing perturbation over the probabilistic watermark decoding. We use D_i ($i = 1, \ldots, n$) to denote the adversary's random delay added to packet P_i. Let $D > 0$ be the maximum of the adversary's random delay, and let σ_d^2 be the variance of all the adversary's ransom delays.

Since the adversary does not know which packets are randomly selected for encoding the watermark, the random selection of those watermark bearing packets P_{z_k} ($k = 1, \ldots, 2r$) is independent from any random delay D_i the adversary could add. Therefore, the impact of the adversary's random delays over randomly selected P_{z_k} is equivalent to randomly choosing one from the random variable list: $D_1, \ldots, D_n$. Let b_k ($k = 1, \ldots, 2r$) denote the impact of the adversary's random delay over the k-th randomly selected packet P_{z_k}. Then b_k has a compound distribution that depends on the probability that each D_i would be selected.

Because each P_{z_k} is randomly chosen according to the same probability distribution from packet list $P_1, \ldots, P_n$, each b_k has the same compound distribution. Furthermore, b_k is also independent from each other as each P_{z_k} is selected independently. In other words, the impact of the adversary's random delays those independently and randomly selected watermark bearing packets is independent and identically distributed (*iid*), and b_k is essentially an *iid* random sample from the random delays the adversary added to all packets.

We use random variables $x_{1,k}$ and $x_{2,k}$ to denote the impact of the adversary's delay over $ipd_{1,k,d}$ and $ipd_{2,k,d}$ respectively. Given b_k is *iid*, we have $x_{1,k}, x_{2,k} \in [-D, D]$, $E(x_{1,k}) = E(x_{2,k}) = 0$, and $Var(x_{1,k}) = Var(x_{2,k}) = 2\sigma_d^2$ and both $x_{1,k}$ and $x_{2,k}$ are *iid*. Let $X_k = \frac{(x_{1,k} - x_{2,k})}{2}$, then X_k is *iid*, $E(X_k) = 0$, and $Var(X_k) = \sigma_d^2$.

We use random variable $Y_{k,d}'$ to denotes the resulting value of $Y_{k,d}$ after it is perturbed by $x_{1,k}$ and $x_{2,k}$, then we have

$$
\begin{aligned}
Y_{k,d}' &= \frac{(ipd_{1,k,d} + x_{1,k}) - (ipd_{2,k,d} + x_{2,k})}{2} \\
&= \frac{(ipd_{1,k,d} - ipd_{2,k,d})}{2} + \frac{(x_{1,k} - x_{2,k})}{2} \\
&= Y_{k,d} + X_k
\end{aligned}
\tag{4.33}
$$

Given $E(Y_{k,d}) = 0$ and $E(X_k) = 0$, we have $E(Y_{k,d}') = 0$. Since both $Y_{k,d}$ and X_k are *iid*, $Y_{k,d}'$ is also *iid*.

$$
\begin{aligned}
Var(Y_{k,d}') &= Var(Y_{k,d}) + Var(X_k) + 2Cov(Y_{k,d}, X_k) \\
&= \sigma_{Y,d}^2 + \sigma_d^2 + 2Cor(Y_{k,d}, X_k)\sigma_{Y,d}\sigma_d \\
&\leq \sigma_{Y,d}^2 + \sigma_d^2 + 2\sigma_{Y,d}\sigma_d \\
&= (\sigma_{Y,d} + \sigma_d)^2
\end{aligned}
\tag{4.34}
$$

We use random variable $\overline{Y_{r,d}'}$ to denote the resulting value of $\overline{Y_{r,d}}$ after it is perturbed by $x_{1,k}$ and $x_{2,k}$, then we have

$$
\overline{Y_{r,d}'} = \frac{1}{r} \sum_{k=1}^{r} Y_{k,d}'
\tag{4.35}
$$

Given that $Y_{k,d}'$s is *iid* and $E(Y_{k,d}') = 0$ (for $k = 1, \ldots, r$), we have $E(\overline{Y_{r,d}'}) = 0$ and $Var(\overline{Y_{r,d}'}) = \frac{Var(Y_{k,d}')}{r}$.

By applying the Central Limit Theorem to random sample $Y_{1,d}', \ldots, Y_{r,d}'$, where $E(Y_{k,d}') = 0$, we have

$$
Pr[\frac{\sqrt{r}(\overline{Y_{r,d}'} - E(Y_{k,d}'))}{\sqrt{Var(Y_{k,d}')}} < x] = Pr[\frac{\sqrt{r}\overline{Y_{r,d}'}}{\sqrt{Var(Y_{k,d}')}} < x]
$$

$$
= \Phi(x)
\tag{4.36}
$$

Therefore

$$\Pr[\overline{Y'_{r,d}} < a] = \Pr[\frac{\sqrt{r}\overline{Y'_{r,d}}}{\sqrt{\mathrm{Var}(Y'_{k,d})}} < \frac{a\sqrt{r}}{\sqrt{\mathrm{Var}(Y'_{k,d})}}]$$

$$\approx \Phi(\frac{a\sqrt{r}}{\sqrt{\mathrm{Var}(Y'_{k,d})}}) \qquad (4.37)$$

$$= \Phi(\frac{a\sqrt{r}}{\sqrt{\sigma_{Y,d}^2 + \sigma_d^2 + 2\mathrm{Cor}(Y_{k,d}, X_k)\sigma_{Y,d}\sigma_d}})$$

$$\geq \Phi(\frac{a\sqrt{r}}{\sigma_{Y,d} + \sigma_d})$$

Equation (4.37) gives us an accurate estimate of the probability of correct watermark bit decoding in the presence of timing perturbation by the adversary. The correlation coefficient $\mathrm{Cor}(Y_{k,d}, X_k)$, whose value range is $[-1, 1]$, models any correlation between the adversary's timing perturbation and the inter-packet timing of the original packet flow.

The important result here is that no matter how large the variance of $Y_{k,d}$ may be (as long as it is finite), no matter how large the variance of the adversary's timing perturbation may be, no matter how small the watermark encoding timing adjustment $a > 0$ (i.e., the encoded watermark signal strength) might be, we can always make the correct watermark bit decoding probability arbitrarily close to 100 % by increasing the redundancy number r. This result holds true regardless of the distribution of the random delays by the adversary.

4.3.3 Advantages Over Quantization Based Flow Watermarking

Unlike the quantization based flow watermarking scheme described in Sect. 4.2, the probabilistic flow watermarking scheme never guarantees 100 % probability of correct watermark decoding from the watermarked packet flow even without any perturbation. On the other hand, the quantization based flow watermarking scheme guarantees 100 % probability of correct watermark decoding from the watermarked flow when there is no distortion. In this section, we show that the probabilistic flow watermarking scheme is actually superior to the quantization based flow watermarking scheme in the presence of timing perturbation.

To fairly compare the performance of the quantization based flow watermarking and the probabilistic watermarking in the presence of timing perturbation, we need to evaluate them under the same condition: (1) the same average timing distortion for encoding the watermark; (2) the same timing distortion by the adversary; and (3) the same number of packets delayed to encode the watermark.

Equation (4.18) shows the expected probability of correct watermark bit decoding by the quantization based flow watermarking scheme an average delay s on m randomly selected packets under timing perturbation of variance σ^2.

Equation (4.37) shows the expected probability of correct watermark bit decoding by the probabilistic flow watermarking scheme with an average delay a on $2r$ randomly selected packets under timing perturbation of variance σ_d^2. Unlike the quantization based flow watermarking scheme, the correct watermark bit decoding probability of the probabilistic flow watermarking scheme depends on not only the variance of the timing perturbation σ_d^2 but also the variance of the difference of the IPD of the original flow $\sigma_{Y,d}^2$.

Figure 4.8 shows the expected correct watermark bit decoding probability of both the quantization based flow watermarking scheme and the probabilistic flow watermarking scheme with an average 200 ms delay on 10, 12, 14, 16, 18, 20, 22, 24, 26 packets under the same timing perturbation of standard deviation 288.68 ms. For the probabilistic flow watermarking scheme, we assume the standard deviation of the IPD difference $\sigma_{Y,d}^2 = 50$. It clearly shows that the probabilistic flow watermarking scheme is much more robust against the timing perturbation than the quantization based flow watermarking scheme under the same conditions. Specifically, when the watermark bit is encoded with an average 200 ms delay on 10 packets, the probabilistic flow watermarking scheme has 90.67 % probability to decode the watermark bit correctly under a timing perturbation of standard deviation 288.68 ms. Under the same condition, quantization based flow watermarking scheme has only 56.14 % probability to decode the watermark bit correctly. In fact, even if we

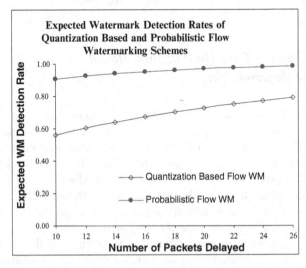

Fig. 4.8 Comparison of expected probability of correct watermark decoding of quantization based and probabilistic flow watermarking

increase the standard deviation of the IPD difference $\sigma^2_{Y,d}$ from 50 to 500, the probabilistic flow watermarking scheme still has better correct watermark decoding probability than the quantization based flow watermarking scheme under the same level of timing perturbation. Therefore, the probabilistic flow watermarking scheme is inherently more robust and effective than the quantization based flow watermarking scheme in the presence of timing perturbation.

4.4 Countermeasures Against Active Timing Based Traceback

In previous sections, we have shown that active timing based approaches are effective in correlating encrypted traffic in the presence of timing perturbation. However, the quantization based and the probabilistic flow watermarking approaches assume no packet added or dropped in the packet flows to be correlated, and they are not effective if there are packets added or dropped.

As a countermeasure to active timing based traceback, attackers could deliberately add bogus packets to or drop some packets from the encrypted traffic. This will change not only the number of packets but also the inter-packet timing characteristics of the packet flow. For example, to frustrate the active timing based traceback, an attacker can add $n > 1$ bogus packets or chaff to an encrypted packet flow of n packets. The bogus packets not only decreased the average inter-packet arrival time to half of that of the original packet flow, but also make it difficult for the watermark decoder to detect the watermark from the "chaffed" packet flow. Specifically, the watermark decoder can not determine exactly which packet is chaff which packet is the original packet as all the packets are encrypted and appear random. In other words, the watermark decoder can not pinpoint those packets that have been used for embedding the watermark, thus it is hard to detect the watermark from the chaffed packet flow.

Blum et al. [8] analyzed the impact of chaff to the correlation of encrypted packet flows and they claimed the hardness result: "when the attacker can insert chaff that is more than a certain threshold fraction, the attacker can make the attacking streams mimic two independent random processes, and thus completely evade any detection algorithm." They further claimed that their "hardness analysis will apply even when the monitor can actively manipulate the timing delay."

The hardness claim by [8] essentially says that adding enough chaff would defeat any timing based correlation methods. This seems intuitively right as it would be almost impossible to recover any original timing characteristics from a packet flow overwhelmed with bogus packets. If this is true, chaff would be a fundamental obstacle to the traceback. On the other hand, it suggests a simple way of achieving anonymity.

Chapter 5
Anonymity

5.1 The Concept of Anonymity

In general, *anonymity* refers to the state of lack of identity among a set of subjects
– the anonymity set [35]. Anonymity does not exist in isolation but often involves
relation between some subject in the anonymity set, some other object, action or
information, and the adversary who is striving to attribute certain action to the
subject. For example, subject A in the anonymity set may have sent/received a
message to/from subject B. In this context, anonymity implies *unlinkability* between
certain subjects, objects, actions or information from the adversary's perspective.

Specifically, *sender anonymity* means that the identity of the information sender
is hidden even if the identity of the information receiver is known. *Receiver
anonymity* means that the identity of the information receiver is hidden even if the
identity of the information sender is known. *Relationship anonymity* refers to the
unlinkability between the information sender and the receiver. In other words, even
if the adversary can see there are information exchanges among some subjects in the
anonymity set, he just can not figure out exactly who is communicating with whom.

Unobservability means the very existence of the subject or communication
is hidden. Unobservability is stronger than unlinkability in that unobservability
implies unlinkability.

Unlike anonymity, *pseudonymity* means the action or information can be
linked to certain pseudonym, which is not the true identity of the subject. While
pseudonyms could be distinguishable among themselves, one pseudonym could be
shared by multiple subjects. It has been shown that pseudonymity can be achieved
on top of anonymity.

In the network context, the subject in the anonymity set usually refers to some
node in the network. The adversary is normally assumed to be able to observe some
or even all network flows between network nodes. A powerful and active adversary
could even perturb the network flows between selected nodes. The anonymity in

© The Author(s) 2015
X. Wang, D. Reeves, *Traceback and Anonymity*, SpringerBriefs
in Computer Science, DOI 10.1007/978-1-4939-3441-6_5

such a context is about hiding the identity of the node who has sent/received information via some network flows that the adversary has observed or perturbed.

5.2 Ways to Achieve Anonymity and Unobservability

Since anonymity is the state of lacking identity, anonymous communication can only be achieved by removing all the identifying characteristics from the network flows used for anonymous communication. For example, if node A and node B communicate by direct message exchange between A and B, the source IP address and the destination IP address of the messaging packets would identify the two communicating parties. In this case, any adversary who can observe the traffic between A and B can figure out that A and B are communicating to each other as some observed network flow contains the IP addresses of node A and B at the same time. Therefore, any anonymous communication must "unlink" the source/destination IP address of the messaging packets from the communicating parties.

Besides the source/destination IP address of the messages, the adversary can also use the content of the message to link the message to the message sender and receiver by monitoring all the messages the subjects send and receive. Therefore, any anonymous communication must also make sure that the observed content of the message sent by A is different from that of the message received by B such that message content can not be correlated to identify the message sender or receiver.

Two basic techniques are widely used for achieving the above two basic requirements in anonymous communication: (1) laundering traffic through intermediate nodes or stepping stones; (2) encryption of message content. In fact, they are the building blocks that underlie almost all known anonymous communication systems.

By laundering the traffic through some intermediate nodes or stepping stones, no single network flow would contain both IP addresses of the message sender and receiver at the same time. For example, node A can send the anonymous message to some intermediate node C, which forwards the message to node B. In this case, node C functions as the stepping stone between node A and node B. Neither the network flow $f_{A,C}$ from A to C, nor the network flow $f_{C,B}$ from C to B contains the IP addresses of both A and B. Therefore, the adversary only sees that A is communicating with C, and C is communicating with B. Assuming node C is communicating with many nodes, it would be difficult for the adversary to determine whether A is communicating with B unless he can reliably correlate the network flow $f_{A,C}$ with network flow $f_{C,B}$. To make it even harder, node A can launder its traffic through multiple stepping stones (e.g., C, D, and E).

Encrypting the message before sending will make it appear random to the adversary. To prevent correlation the encrypted messages, the message should be encrypted with different keys when it is laundered via different stepping stones. For example, one could use key $K_{A,C}$ to encrypt the messages from node A to node C, and uses key $K_{C,B}$ to encrypt messages from node C to node B. To prevent the adversary from correlating the encrypted messages based on the message length, the message sender could make all sent messages to have the same length by dividing the original message into chunks of same size and adding padding when needed.

5.2.1 MIX and MIX Network

The *mix* proposed by Chaum [10] is essentially a stepping stone that disguises the message content via encryption and other transformations (e.g., fragmentation of the message). Assuming X wants to send an anonymous message M to Y via a mix $\mathcal{M}$, and the public key of X, Y and the mix are x, y and k respectively. X first encrypts the prepending random string R_0 and the message M with Y's public key y, then further encrypts it with prepending random string R_1 and appending address of Y with the mix's public key k. X sends following to the mix:

$$E_k(R_1, E_y(R_0, M), Y) \tag{5.1}$$

The mix decrypts the received message with its private key k^{-1} to obtain $R_1, E_y(R_0, M), Y$. Therefore, only the mix can obtain the receiver's address Y in the received message. The mix will forward $E_y(R_0, M)$ to Y at appropriate time. To disguise the message arrival order, the mix can buffer received messages and send them out in a batch according to certain order. The message sender can make the encrypted message $E_y(R_0, M)$ of the same size to prevent correlation based on message size.

Here the input $(E_k(R_1, E_y(R_0, M), Y))$ and the output $(E_y(R_0, M))$ of the mix are completely different and there is no way to correlate them based on content. Although the mix knows the message sender and the message receiver, it does not have access to the content of message M but only $E_y(R_0, M)$. Apparently, if the mix is compromised, the unlinkability would be broken. Therefore, single mix has single point of failure.

To remove the single point of failure in the mix, multiple mixes can be used together to form a *mix network*. Assume the mix network has n mixes: $\mathcal{M}_1, \ldots, \mathcal{M}_n$ whose public keys are $k_1, \ldots, k_n$ respectively. X prepares the following sealed information to be sent to the first mix in the mix network:

$$E_{k_1}(R_1, E_{k_2}(R_2, \ldots, E_{k_{n-1}}(R_{n-1}, E_{k_n}(R_n, E_y(R_0, M), Y), \mathcal{M}_n) \ldots, \mathcal{M}_3), \mathcal{M}_2) \tag{5.2}$$

From the encrypted message received, each mix in the mix network only knows the next hop to which the decrypted message should be forwarded. Without help from others, the mix has no knowledge about where the forwarded message comes from before it reaches the previous mix and where the forwarded message will be further forwarded or delivered. Therefore, as long as there is at least one mix not compromised, the mix network will provide some level of anonymity.

5.2.2   *Dinning Cryptographer Network and Anonymous Buses*

While anonymity requires unlinkability between the protected subjects and certain action, it does not necessarily hide all the sensitive actions (e.g., communicating with the network). In other words, the anonymity system just needs to make sure the adversary is unable to figure out who is communicating with who, and it does not necessarily prevent the adversary from observing who is communicating with the network. By identifying who are communicating at the same time, the adversary could potentially narrow down the anonymity set and break the anonymity. Unobservability provides stronger protection by preventing the adversary from identifying who is actually communicating at all.

Assume the adversary is able to observe who is sending or receiving information to/from the network, one simple way to achieve unobservability is to hide the real communication within constant-rated, random cover traffic. All the real messages will be encrypted and of the same fixed size. All the subjects are to send and receive random messages of the same fixed size of the real messages if they are not sending and receiving the real messages. If all the subjects send and receive constant-rate traffic at the same time, it is infeasible for the adversary to determine who has ever sent or received actual messages.

Apparently, it is impractical to have many subjects to send and receive constant rate traffic at the same time. The *Dinning Cryptographer Network* (DC-Net) [11] proposed by Chaum enables one to anonymously transmit one bit without constant-rate cover traffic.

Assume there are n cryptographers $c_0, c_1, \ldots, c_{n-1}$ sitting in a circle, each c_i secretly generates a random bit $x_{i,(i+1)\%n}$ and secretly share it to the neighbor $c_{(i+1)\%n}$. Let s_i be c_i's secret bit indicating whether c_i has secretly paid the meal. Each c_i broadcasts value $z_i = x_{(i+n-1)\%n,i} \oplus x_{i,(i+1)\%n} \oplus s_i$ to everyone. Then the exclusive sum of all the broadcasted bits would be $Z = z_0 \oplus \ldots \oplus z_{n-1} = s_0 \oplus \ldots \oplus s_{n-1}$.

If no more than one cryptographer has secretly paid for the meal, and every cryptographer is honest, then Z will accurately indicate whether one of the cryptographer has secretly paid the bill. Since every cryptographer c_i has sent and received exactly the same amount of random looking traffic, there is no way to tell which cryptographer has secretly paid the meal by simply monitoring the traffic to/from each cryptographer. Therefore, the DC-net allows one to anonymously send one bit to the public.

However, the two neighbors of any cryptographer c_i could collude to reveal if c_i has secretly paid the meal. The two neighbors just need to combine their shared secrets $x_{(i+n-1)\%n,i}$, and $x_{i,(i+1)\%n}$ with the broadcasted z_i to obtain c_i's secret value s_i.

$$z_i \oplus x_{(i+n-1)\%n,i} \oplus x_{i,(i+1)\%n} \tag{5.3}$$

$$= (x_{(i+n-1)\%n,i} \oplus x_{i,(i+1)\%n} \oplus s_i) \oplus x_{(i+n-1)\%n,i} \oplus x_{i,(i+1)\%n}$$

$$= s_i$$

Another fundamental issue of D-Net is that it only allow one participating node to communicate at a time. As a result, any participating cryptographer can corrupt the whole DC-Net channel completely by broadcasting random bits.

Anonymous buses [6] utilize a bus that has n^2 seats to carry messages between n nodes. Conceptually, the bus traverses the n nodes and stops at each node to pick up and deliver messages among the n nodes. If node i wants to send a message to node j, it encrypts the message with node j's public key and loads the encrypted message to seat $s_{i,j}$ when the bus stops at node i. Otherwise, it simply loads random bit to seat $s_{i,j}$. When the bus arrives at node j, it tries to decrypt the content of seat $s_{i,j}$ with its private key. From the adversary's perspective, every node upload some random looking data to n seats and read some random looking data from n seats. Since the adversary is not able to distinguish whether the random looking data is real message or random data, it can not tell if any node has sent or received any real message.

Unlike DC-Net, anonymous bus allows multiple nodes to communicate anonymously at the same time. It has $O(n)$ computation complexity and $O(n^2)$ storage complexity.

Similar to DC-Net, anonymous bus is fragile. An active adversary can corrupt the whole anonymous bus channel by simply overwriting selected seats with random data.

5.3 Proposed Anonymity Systems

Ever since Chaum developed the mix concept [10] and the DC-Net concept [11], many anonymity systems have been proposed based on either the MIX or cover traffic.

From anonymous communication's perspective, anonymity systems can be categorized into (1) high-latency systems and (2) low-latency systems.

5.3.1 High-Latency Anonymity Systems

High-latency anonymity systems are designed to provide anonymity to non-interactive applications such as email that can tolerate long delays. The original MIX proposed by Chaum [10] was intended for email with high latency.

Anon.penet.fi [23] is a pseudonymity remailer that replaces email sender's real email address with a pseudonym. It forwards the email to its intended recipient after stripping the identifying information from the email message. By keeping the mapping between the real email address and the pseudonym, anon.penet.fi allows email recipient to reply back to the real email sender based on pseudonym.

Similar to the mix network, cypherpunk remailer [1] choose a sequence of servers through which the email will be forwarded. It uses multiple layers of encryption with next hop's public key. This makes sure that each intermediate server has no knowledge about where the email will be forwarded by the next hop. Unlike mix network, cypherpunk remailer adds neither random padding nor any explicit batching and delay. This make it susceptible to correlation based on packet size and timing.

Mixmaster [28] is another (i.e., type II) remailer that uses intermediate nodes to relay encrypted and anonymized email messages. Unlike cypherpunk remailer, mixmaster sends messages of fixed-size and it changes the order of messages. This makes it infeasible to correlate the anonymized messages based on message size. However, mixmaster does not support anonymous reply.

Mixminion [14] is yet another mix network based (i.e., type III) remailer that addresses several shortcomings of mixmaster. It allows anonymous reply and uses key rotation to provide better resistance against replay attacks.

5.3.2 Low-Latency Anonymity Systems

Low-latency anonymity systems are designed to support real-time (or near real-time), interactive applications. While low-latency anonymity systems are also built upon the concept of mix, their buffering delay has to be small due to the low-latency requirement. Consequently, low-latency anonymity systems have much less batching and reordering of messages than high-latency anonymity systems. The intermediate node in low-latency anonymity systems are usually called proxy rather than mix. To reduce the processing overhead, low-latency anonymity systems minimize the use of asymmetric encryption and instead use symmetric encryption when possible.

Anonymizer.com [3] is a commercial anonymity service provider that anonymizes web browsing traffic. It accepts web browsing requests via SSH tunnel from its clients, and it replaces the client's IP address in each browsing request with the IP address of anonymizer's proxy before forwarding the browsing request to its destination. Therefore, the anonymized web browsing request appears from anonymizer's proxy. In addition, anonymizer filters out adware from the web traffic and returns the filtered web traffic back to its client via the SSH tunnel.

Onion routing [45] is a free low-latency anonymity system that anonymizes traffic via a number of intermediate application level proxies called *onion routers*. Similar to the mix in a mix network, each onion router maintains a private and public key pair. The user of onion routing chooses a sequence of onion routers and constructs separate encryption tunnel to each of the chosen onion routers. The multi-layer tunnelling represents the path or *circuit* the anonymized message will go through. Unlike traditional mix network, onion routing only uses asymmetric cryptography to setup the circuit, and it uses faster symmetric cryptography once the circuit has been setup.

Tor [17] is the second generation onion routing. It has introduced directory service, better circuit establishment against replay attack and location hidden services. However, it has been demonstrated [32] that the adversary can identify the true location of Tor's hidden service.

Crowds [46] seeks to anonymize web browsing traffic by laundering the traffic via randomly chosen intermediate nodes. Each node simply forward the web browsing traffic to a randomly chosen intermediate node with probability $0.5 < p < 1$. Unlike onion routing or Tor, the intermediate node in crowds does not encrypt the forwarded traffic.

Java Anonymous Proxy (JAP) [7] is another proxy based system to anonymize web browsing traffic. JAP allows user to choose which intermediate nodes to use, and it generate dummy traffic as an effort to thwart traffic analysis.

Tarzan [19] is a peer-to-peer anonymous network layer based on tunnelling across multiple intermediate nodes. It supports UDP and uses cover traffic to disguise the anonymized traffic.

MorphMix [47] is a peer-to-peer anonymity system that aims to address several shortcomings of static mix networks. It proposed collusion detection to address the collusion attacks by malicious nodes. Later it has been shown [57] that the proposed collusion detection is not effective.

P5 [51] uses cover traffic to anonymize traffic. Instead of using constant cover traffic from every node to every other node, P5 groups users into tree-structured *broadcast groups*, and only broadcast encrypted traffic to selected groups. Since it requires each user to generate constant rate cover traffic, it is unlikely to be practical.

5.4 Interaction Between Traceback and Anonymity

In the network context, anonymity is often referred as anonymous communication. The goal of anonymous communication system is to hide the identity of the sender, receiver of anonymized network flow or conceal the relationship between the communicating parties. On the other hand, the goal of traceback is to recover the real source of the attack traffic and the identity of the attacker. Therefore, the goals of anonymous communication and traceback are in direct conflict!

No matter how anonymous communication conceals the information exchange between anonymous parties, the information exchange exists. In the network context, this means there exists transmission of information between potentially anonymous network nodes. we model the information transmission path between network nodes as the *network information flow*. Here the transmission could have multiple sources and/or multiple destinations. Therefore a network information flow is not necessarily linear (e.g., multi-cast or broadcast) and it may consists of multiple network flows each of which has single source and destination. For example, node A may send information to node B via network flow $f_{A,B}$. Node B may send 50 % of the received information from A to node C via network flow $f_{B,C}$ and the rest 50 % to node D via network flow $f_{B,D}$. The network information flow between nodes A, B, C, and D consists of three network flows $f_{A,B}$, $f_{B,C}$, and $f_{B,D}$. Therefore, the hidden information transmission in anonymous communication can be modelled by the network information flow.

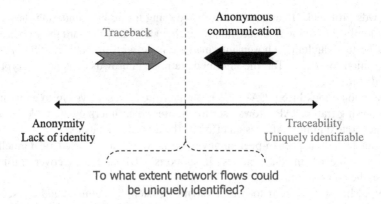

Fig. 5.1 Tradeoff between Traceback and Anonymity

If the hidden information transmission is not disguised by constant cover traffic from all participating nodes, then identifying the corresponding network information flow would usually reveal the hidden information source and destination thus break the anonymity.

As we have show in previous chapters, traceback techniques have become increasingly powerful in that they can handle more and more attack flow disguise techniques (e.g., stepping stones, encryption, timing perturbation). On the other hand, more and more anonymity techniques have been proposed to provide anonymity despite countermeasures. Therefore, there is a tradeoff between the traceback and anonymity techniques as illustrated in Fig. 5.1.

It is very unlikely that there exist any technique that can provide absolute anonymity in that no traceback technique can break its anonymity. It is equally unlikely there exist any traceback technique that can break the anonymity of any anonymity system. There must exist some technical limit on how much traceback and anonymity techniques can do. The open questions are:

• To what extent can traceback technique recover the source and path of anonymized attack flow given all possible anonymity techniques?
• To what extent can we anonymize a network flow given all possible traceback techniques?

In the next chapter, we present research results that help answer these fundamental questions.

Chapter 6
Fundamental Limitations in Low-Latency Anonymity Systems

There are two major types of adversaries against low-latency anonymity systems: (1) passive; and (2) active. The passive adversary is assumed to be able to observe part or all communication traffic between network nodes without changing anything of the observed traffic. The active adversary, on the other hand, is assumed to be able to change or perturb, in addition to observing, traffic between network nodes. Since the active adversary is more powerful than the passive adversary, the two types of adversaries may lead to fundamentally different limitations of low-latency anonymity systems. Therefore, we will examine the impact of two types of adversaries separately.

6.1 Limitations of Low-Latency Anonymity Systems Against Passive Adversary

If the anonymity system uses neither dummy traffic nor broadcasting, then an omnipresent passive adversary can break the unlinkability with enough observations even if all the messages are of the same size and encrypted [26]. This is not surprising if an omnipresent adversary can observe all and only those message transfers between all senders and receivers.

To make it harder for the omnipresent passive adversary to figure out who is communicating with whom, many proposed anonymity systems (e.g., Web-MIXes [7], Hordes [52], Netcamo [21], Tarzan [19]) use dummy traffic to cover the real traffic to be anonymized. When the message of the dummy traffic is encrypted and of the same size as that of the real traffic, it is practically indistinguishable from the real traffic from the adversary's perspective. In this case, it is infeasible to identify and track the anonymized network flow based on the content or size of the packet or message.

© The Author(s) 2015
X. Wang, D. Reeves, *Traceback and Anonymity*, SpringerBriefs
in Computer Science, DOI 10.1007/978-1-4939-3441-6_6

Even if all the messages are encrypted and are of the same size, each message is sent and received at different time at any given node. Previous research has shown that inter-packet timing is largely preserved across routers and stepping stones. Therefore, if the anonymized packet flow has unique inter-packet timing characteristics, it can be exploited by the adversary to break the unlinkability and anonymity. Specifically, timing attack seeks to uniquely identify, track anonymized packet flow by analyzing the inter-packet timing of packet flows. Since timing attack is based on packet timing only, it is applicable even if the packet (or message) is encrypted and of fixed size.

Information theoretic analysis [61] shows that appropriate level of cover traffic (i.e., dummy message) can protect the anonymity from passive timing attack if the inter-packet timing follows unit-rate Poisson processes.

Work [8] analyzed the impact of cover traffic (i.e., chaff) to the correlation of encrypted packet flows and they claimed the hardness result: "when the attacker can insert chaff that is more than a certain threshold fraction, the attacker can make the attacking streams mimic two independent random processes, and thus completely evade any detection algorithm." The authors further claimed that their "hardness analysis will apply even when the monitor can actively manipulate the timing delay."

The hardness result by work [8] essentially claims that adding enough chaff (or the cover traffic) would make it impossible to distinguish and identify the anoymized flow from others even if the adversary can actively perturb the inter-packet timing. Because the chaff packets can be encrypted and have the same size of the original packets, it is infeasible for the adversary to distinguish the encrypted chaff packets from the original encrypted packets. When overwhelmingly large amount of chaff (e.g., 10 times more than the original packets) are added to the anoymized packet flow, the inter-packet timing of the packet flow would be dominated by the chaff and would become very different from the original. Just as it is hard to track and identify a person inside a crowded mall, it is difficult to track and identify any anoymized packet flow buried in overwhelmingly large amount of chaff.

The key question here is: whether the hardness claim by work [8] holds true against active adversary who can actively perturb the inter-packet timing to make it easier to identify the packet flow.

6.2   Limitations of Low-Latency Anonymity Systems Against Active Adversary

Work [27] shows that cover traffic can be effective against passive timing analysis, but it is not effective against a more active timing attack that drops selected packets. This suggests that the hardness result by work [8] might be wrong in the presence of active adversary.

Since dropping selected packets is essentially the opposite of adding chaff or cover traffic, one might think it is the weakening of chaff due to selected packet dropping that has rendered adding chaff ineffective against packet dropping based timing attacks. The question is: whether adding cover traffic is effective against those active timing attacks that do not drop and weaken the cover traffic?

In Chap. 4, we have presented two schemes that can transparently watermark given packet flows, and we have shown that they are robust against timing perturbation. However, those two flow watermarking schemes are not effective against chaff or cover traffic. Specifically, the decoding of those two flow watermark schemes requires the exact knowledge of which packets have been used for encoding/decoding the watermark. Adding chaff or cover traffic would make it infeasible for the decoder to determine exactly which (encrypted) packets have been used for encoding/decoding the watermark, thus would disrupt the watermark decoding. In order to make the flow watermarking robust against adding chaff or cover traffic, the watermark encoding and decoding must not depend on any specific packets.

To address the issues caused by cover traffic or chaff, researchers have designed a new flow watermarking scheme based on the concept of centroid [63]. Specifically, the watermark bit is encoded/decoded upon the centroid of a set of packets instead of specific individual packets. When the set size is large (i.e., there are many packets in the set), adding or dropping a few packets to or from the set does not change the centroid much. This enables us to reliably decode the watermark even if substantial chaff or cover traffic has been added to the watermarked packet flow.

6.2.1 Time Interval and Centroid of Time Interval

Given a packet flow of duration $T_f > 0$, we divide the whole duration of the packet flow into time intervals of fixed size T ($T > 0$), and we want to embed a l-bit watermark with redundancy $r > 0$. Assume the packet flow duration is long enough such that $T_f > o + 2nT$ where $o > 0$ is the offset from the beginning time of the packet flow and $n = r \times l$. Let t_0 be the absolute time stamp at offset o. Assume there are $n_t > 0$ packets $P_1, \ldots, P_{n_t}$ in time duration $[o, o + 2nT)$, and we use t_i ($i = 1, \ldots, n_t$) to denote the absolute time stamp of packet P_i. We divide the time duration $[o, o + 2nT)$ into $2n$ intervals of length T: $I_0, \ldots, I_{2n-1}$. Then $t_i' = t_i - t_0$ is the relative time of P_i from the beginning of the first interval at offset o, and packet P_i would fall within time interval $\lfloor t_i'/T \rfloor$.

Given any packet P_i, its relative position within its time interval (i.e., offset from the starting point of its time interval) is

$$\Delta t_i = t_i' \bmod T \tag{6.1}$$

Therefore, it is essentially a modulo operation to divide a duration $[o, o+2nT)$ of a packet flow into equally sized intervals, and any packet's relative positions within its time interval is essentially the remainder of the modulo operation on the packet's time stamp in duration $[o, o + 2nT)$.

Given any ordered sequence of time stamps $t'_1, \ldots, t'_{n_t}$ within duration $[o, o + 2nT)$ and a random interval length $T > 0$, no matter what distribution the ordered sequence of time stamps may have, it has been shown [63] that $\Delta t_i = t'_i \bmod T$ is approximately uniformly distributed in range $[0, T)$ when $T \ll t'_{n_t} - t'_1$ and n is large. In other words, given any sufficiently long flow with enough packets, the relative positions of all packets within their respective time intervals (Δt_i) tend to be uniformly distributed. As a result, the expected value of Δt_i is

$$E(\Delta t_i) = \frac{T}{2} \quad (i = 1, \ldots, n) \tag{6.2}$$

and the variance of Δt_i is

$$\text{Var}(\Delta t_i) = \frac{T^2}{12} \quad (i = 1, \ldots, n) \tag{6.3}$$

Given any interval I_i ($i = 0, \ldots, 2n - 1$) that has $n_i > 0$ packets $P_{i_0}, \ldots, P_{i_{n_i-1}}$, we are interested in the "balance point" of those packets in interval I_i, which can be modeled by the *centroid* of interval I_i ($i = 0, \ldots, 2n - 1$):

$$\text{Cent}(I_i) = \frac{1}{n_i} \sum_{j=0}^{n_i-1} \Delta t_{ij} \tag{6.4}$$

In case interval I_i has no packet, we define $\text{Cent}(I_i)$ to be $\frac{T}{2}$. Since $E(\Delta t_{ij}) = \frac{T}{2}$, we have $E(\text{Cent}(I_i)) = \frac{T}{2}$.

6.2.2 Random Grouping of Time Intervals

In order to encode and decode in the inter-packet timing domain, we randomly divide the $2n$ time intervals into two equally sized groups via the following process: we sequentially scan through the $2n$ time intervals and we independently and randomly pick the current time interval to be in group A with probability 0.5. We can expect group A to have n time intervals which are denoted as I_k^A ($k = 0, \ldots, n - 1$). The rest of the n time intervals belong to group B and are denoted as I_k^B ($k = 0, \ldots, n-1$). Figure 6.1 illustrates such a random and equal grouping of the $2n$ time intervals of a given packet flow. It is easy to see that there are $\frac{(2n)!}{n!n!}$ such groupings.

Next we randomly assign r group A intervals and r group B intervals to encode and decode watermark bit i ($i = 0, \ldots, l - 1$). We use $I_{i,j}^A$ and $I_{i,j}^B$ to denote the j-th ($j = 0, \ldots, r - 1$) group A and B interval assigned for watermark

Fig. 6.1 Random grouping of time intervals of packet flow

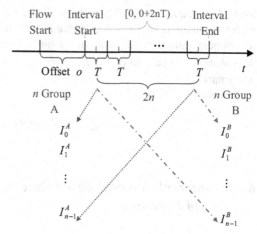

Fig. 6.2 Random assignment of time intervals of packet flow

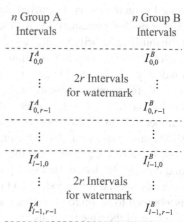

bit i ($i = 0, \ldots, l - 1$). Figure 6.2 illustrates such random assignment of $2n$ time intervals for encoding/decoding l watermark bits with redundancy r. The total number of such assignments is $\frac{n!}{(r!)^l}$.

Let $N_{i,j}^A$ and $N_{i,j}^B$ be the total packet numbers in interval $I_{i,j}^A$ and $I_{i,j}^B$, respectively, and

$$N_i^A = \sum_{j=0}^{r-1} N_{i,j}^A \quad \text{and} \quad N_i^B = \sum_{j=0}^{r-1} N_{i,j}^B$$

Therefore, N_i^A and N_i^B are the total number of packets in group A and B intervals, respectively, assigned for encoding and decoding watermark bit i.

Since each of the $2n$ time intervals is randomly assigned, with equal probability, to group A and B, and each of the group A and B intervals is randomly assigned, with equal probability, for encoding and decoding each of the l watermark bits, each time interval has equal probability to be assigned for each watermark bit. Specifically, each time interval has $\frac{r}{2n} = \frac{1}{2l}$ probability to be one of the $I_{i,j}^A$ ($j = 0, \ldots, r-1$) for encoding and decoding watermark bit i. Similarly, each time interval has $\frac{r}{2n} = \frac{1}{2l}$ probability to be one of the $I_{i,j}^B$ ($j = 0, \ldots, r-1$) for encoding and decoding watermark bit i.

Therefore

$$E(N_i^A) = E(N_i^B) = \frac{n_t}{2l} \tag{6.5}$$

6.2.3 Interval Centroid Based Watermark Encoding and Decoding

Based upon the interval centroid, we can encode arbitrary binary bits into the inter-packet timing domain and make the upper bound of the watermark decoding error probability arbitrarily small for sufficiently long packet flows.

As shown in previous section, given a sufficiently long packet flow, we can randomly group and assign $2r$ intervals $I_{i,j}^A$ and $I_{i,j}^B$ ($j = 0, \ldots, r-1$) of size $T > 0$, from any sufficiently long packet flow, to encode and decode watermark bit i ($i = 0, \ldots, l-1$). Given offset $o > 0$, time interval size $T > 0$ and the number of watermark bits $l > 0$, we use some pseudo random number generator (RNG) and some seed s to do the random grouping and assignment. Therefore, tuple $< o, T, , lRNG, s >$ represents the complete information for the watermark encoder and decoder to derive the exact pseudo random grouping and assignment of time intervals needed for encoding and decoding the l-bit watermark. Such information is assumed to be shared between the encoder and the decoder only.

Once all the time intervals have been pseudo randomly grouped and assigned for the l-bit watermarked, we aggregate all the time stamps in the r group A intervals $I_{i,j}^A$ and the r group B intervals $I_{i,j}^B$. Then we calculate the centroids of those aggregated packets.

Let

$$A_i = \frac{\sum_{j=0}^{r-1}[N_{i,j}^A \mathrm{Cent}(I_{i,j}^A)]}{\sum_{j=0}^{r-1} N_{i,j}^A} \tag{6.6}$$

and

$$B_i = \frac{\sum_{j=0}^{r-1}[N_{i,j}^B \mathrm{Cent}(I_{i,j}^B)]}{\sum_{j=0}^{r-1} N_{i,j}^B} \tag{6.7}$$

Here, A_i and B_i are centroids of all those group A packets (in intervals $I_{i,j}^A$, $j = 0, \ldots, r-1$) and group B packets (in intervals $I_{i,j}^B$, $j = 0, \ldots, r-1$) that are randomly assigned for encoding and decoding watermark bit i.

Since $E(\mathrm{Cent}(I_{i,j}^A)) = E(\mathrm{Cent}(I_{i,j}^A)) = \frac{T}{2}$, we have

$$E(A_i) = E(B_i) = \frac{T}{2} \tag{6.8}$$

Let

$$Y_i = A_i - B_i \tag{6.9}$$

then $E(Y_i) = 0$. This allows us to encode and decode watermark bit i into the difference between A_i and B_i.

To encode bit '1', we can make $E(Y_i) > 1$ by deliberately increasing A_i. To encode bit '0', we can make $E(Y_i) < 1$ by deliberately increasing B_i. The increase of A_i or B_i can be achieved by simply delaying each packet within each $I_{i,j}^A$ or $I_{i,j}^B$ interval.

Let $P_{i,j,k}$ be the k-th packet in interval $I_{i,j}$ (the j-th interval for the i-th watermark bit), $0 < a < T$ be the maximum delay, and $\Delta t_{i,j,k}$ be packet $P_{i,j,k}$'s offset from the start of its interval $I_{i,j}$. We delay packet $P_{i,j,k}$ for a duration of $a - \frac{a\Delta t_{i,j,k}}{T}$ long, which will result the new offset of packet $P_{i,j,k}$

$$\Delta t'_{i,j,k} = a + \frac{(T-a)\Delta t_{i,j,k}}{T} \tag{6.10}$$

It has been proved [63] that above delay strategy essentially "squeezes" the original uniform distribution of $\Delta t_{i,j,k}$ from range $[0, T)$ to range $[a, T)$ as illustrated in Fig. 6.3.

We use random variables A_i' and B_i' to denote the resulting values of A_i and B_i, respectively, after all the packets in intervals $I_{i,j}^A$ and $I_{i,j}^B$ ($j = 0, \ldots, r-1$) have been delayed according to Eq. 6.10. Then we have

Fig. 6.3 Probability distribution of $\Delta t_{i,j,k}$ before and after watermark encoding delay

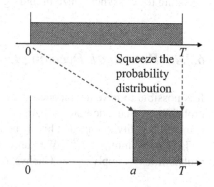

Fig. 6.4 Encoding
watermark bit by shifting the
distribution of Y_i

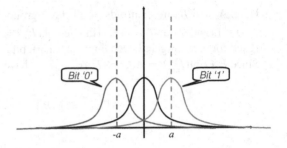

$$E(A_i') = E(B_i') = \frac{T + a}{2} \tag{6.11}$$

Let $Y_i^1 = A_i' - B_i$ and $Y_i^0 = A_i - B_i'$, we have

$$E(Y_i^1) = \frac{a}{2} \quad \text{and} \quad E(Y_i^0) = -\frac{a}{2} \tag{6.12}$$

Therefore, the watermark encoding essentially shifts the distribution of Y_i to the left or right for $\frac{a}{2}$ as illustrated in Fig. 6.4

To decode the watermark from a given flow, we first obtain the exact interval grouping and assignment from the same offset o, interval size T and the seed for the pseudo-random number generator used in watermark encoding. Then we calculate each Y_i $(i = 0, \ldots, l - 1)$. If $Y_i > 0$ then the decoding of watermark bit i is 1; otherwise, the decoding of watermark bit i is 0.

In reality, the correct offset for decoding the watermark from the received packet flow could be different from the original offset due to clock skew, packet delay jitter and all kinds of transformations (e.g., repacketizeation, flow mixing) and perturbations (e.g., deliberate packet drop, delay) that interfere with the packet timing. Since the distribution Y_i is symmetric around zero, decoding with any wrong offset tends to be random such that about 50 % of the l-bit watermark will be matched. As shown in Fig. 6.5, the decoding will have most bits matched only with the right offset (10 s in the Figure). This property allows our flow watermark decoding to self-synchronize in finding the right offset to decode.

6.2.4 Watermark Decoding Error Probability Analysis

It is possible to have an encoded watermark bit decoded wrong. $\Pr[Y_i^0 > 0]$ is the probability of encoded bit '0' being mistakenly decoded as bit '1', and $\Pr[Y_i^1 \leq 0]$ is the probability of encoded bit '1' being mistakenly decoded as bit '0'.

Let $N_i = \min(N_i^A, N_i^B)$. We can derive an upper bound of the decoding error probabilities by applying the Chebyshev inequality to Y_i^0 and Y_i^1,

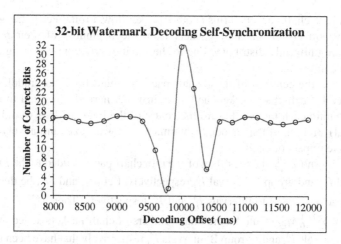

Fig. 6.5 Decoding with different offsets

$$\Pr[|Y_i^1 - E(Y_i^1)| \geq \frac{a}{2}] \leq \frac{4\text{Var}(Y_i^1)}{a^2} \leq \frac{T^2 + (T-a)^2}{3a^2 N_i} \quad (6.13)$$

Because the distribution of $\Pr[Y_i^1 - \frac{a}{2}]$ is symmetric

$$\Pr[Y_i^1 < 0] = \frac{1}{2}\Pr[|Y_i^1 - E(Y_i^1)| \geq \frac{a}{2}] \leq \frac{T^2 + (T-a)^2}{6a^2 N_i} \quad (6.14)$$

Similarly, we have

$$\Pr[Y_i^0 > 0] \leq \frac{T^2 + (T-a)^2}{6a^2 N_i} \quad (6.15)$$

Therefore, given any sufficiently long packet flow with enough packets, we can always make the decoding error probability arbitrarily close to zero by increasing N_i, which can be achieved by increasing the redundancy number r.

6.2.4.1   Robustness Against Chaff and Flow Mixing

Now we analyze the robustness of the centroid interval based watermark decoding against chaff and flow mixing. Here we consider any packets added to or mixed with a given packet flow n packets: $P_1, \ldots, P_n$ as *chaff*. Assume there are totally m chaff packets $P_{c,1}, \ldots, P_{c,m}$ added to the original packet flow. The resulting flow would have $n + m$ packets: $P_1', \ldots, P_{m+n}'$ (P_i' is either P_j or $P_{c,j}$) is a mix of the original flow and the chaff.

Here all the chaff packets forms another packet flow. From Sect. 6.2.1, we know the relative offsets of all chaff packets from the beginning of their respective intervals are uniformly distributed due to the random grouping and assignment of all the time intervals.

Therefore, the centroid of those chaff packets would be in the middle of each time interval. Such chaff packets added to an watermarked flow tend to shift the centroid within each interval toward the center of the interval. This would weaken the (signal) strength of the encoded watermark. We want to quantitatively analyze the negative impact of chaff.

Let $\Delta \hat{t}_{i,j,k}^A$ and $\Delta \hat{t}_{i,j,k}^B$ be the offset of the k-th chaff packet added to the j-th group A interval $I_{i,j}^A$ and group B interval $I_{i,j}^B$ respectively. Let $M_{i,j}^A$ and $M_{i,j}^B$ be the number of chaff packets added to intervals $I_{i,j}^A$ and $I_{i,j}^B$ respectively. Then $M_i^A = \sum_{j=0}^{r-1} M_{i,j}^A$ and $M_i^B = \sum_{j=0}^{r-1} M_{i,j}^B$ would be the total numbers of chaff packets added to those r group A intervals $I_{i,j}^A$ and r group B intervals $I_{i,j}^A$ respectively that have been assigned for encoding and decoding watermark bit i.

Let

$$C_i^A = \frac{\sum_{j=0}^{r-1} \sum_{k=0}^{M_{i,j}^A - 1} \Delta \hat{t}_{i,j,k}^A}{M_i^A} \tag{6.16}$$

and

$$C_i^B = \frac{\sum_{j=0}^{r-1} \sum_{k=0}^{M_{i,j}^B - 1} \Delta \hat{t}_{i,j,k}^B}{M_i^B} \tag{6.17}$$

Because $\Delta \hat{t}_{i,j,k}^A$ and $\Delta \hat{t}_{i,j,k}^B$ are uniformly distributed within intervals $I_{i,j}^A$ and $I_{i,j}^B$ respectively, we have

$$E(C_i^A) = E(C_i^B) = \frac{T}{2} \tag{6.18}$$

$$\mathrm{Var}(C_i^A) \leq \frac{T^2}{12M_i} \tag{6.19}$$

$$\mathrm{Var}(C_i^B) \leq \frac{T^2}{12M_i} \tag{6.20}$$

where $M_i = \min(M_i^A, M_i^B)$.

Now we analyze the impact of those chaff packets over $A_i, B_i, A_i', B_i', Y_i^0, Y_i^1$ and the watermark decoding error probability $\Pr[Y_i^0 > 0]$ and $\Pr[Y_i^1 < 0]$.

Let $\hat{A}_i$ and $\hat{B}_i$ be the random variables that denote the resulting values of A_i and B_i respectively after chaff has been added. We have

$$\hat{A}_i = \frac{\sum_{j=0}^{r-1} \sum_{k=0}^{N_{i,j}^A-1} \Delta t_{i,j,k}^A + \sum_{j=0}^{r-1} \sum_{k=0}^{M_{i,j}^A-1} \Delta \hat{t}_{i,j,k}^A}{N_i^A + M_i^A} = \frac{N_i^A A_i + M_i^A C_i^A}{N_i^A + M_i^A} \tag{6.21}$$

$$\hat{B}_i = \frac{\sum_{j=0}^{r-1} \sum_{k=0}^{N_{i,j}^B-1} \Delta t_{i,j,k}^B + \sum_{j=0}^{r-1} \sum_{k=0}^{M_{i,j}^B-1} \Delta \hat{t}_{i,j,k}^B}{N_i^B + M_i^B} = \frac{N_i^B B_i + M_i^B C_i^B}{N_i^B + M_i^B} \tag{6.22}$$

$$E(\hat{A}_i) = E(\hat{B}_i) = \frac{T}{2} \tag{6.23}$$

$$\text{Var}(\hat{A}_i) = \frac{T^2}{12(N_i^A + M_i^A)} \tag{6.24}$$

$$\text{Var}(\hat{B}_i) = \frac{T^2}{12(N_i^B + M_i^B)} \tag{6.25}$$

Let $\hat{A}_i'$ and $\hat{B}_i'$ be the random variables that denote the resulting values of A_i' and B_i' respectively after chaff has been added. We have

$$E(\hat{A}_i') = \frac{N_i^A E(A_i') + M_i^A E(C_i^A)}{N_i^A + M_i^A} = \frac{T}{2} + \frac{aN_i^A}{2(N_i^A + M_i^A)} \tag{6.26}$$

$$E(\hat{B}_i') = \frac{N_i^B E(B_i') + M_i^B E(C_i^A)}{N_i^B + M_i^B} = \frac{T}{2} + \frac{aN_i^B}{2(N_i^B + M_i^B)} \tag{6.27}$$

$$\text{Var}(\hat{A}_i') = \frac{N_i^A(T-a)^2 + M_i^A T^2}{12(N_i^A + M_i^A)^2} \tag{6.28}$$

$$\text{Var}(\hat{B}_i') = \frac{N_i^B(T-a)^2 + M_i^B T^2}{12(N_i^B + M_i^B)^2} \tag{6.29}$$

We use random variables $\hat{Y}_i^0$ and $\hat{Y}_i^1$ to denote the resulting values of Y_i^0 and Y_i^1 respectively after the chaff packets have been added. We have

$$E(\hat{Y}_i^0) = E(\hat{A}_i) - E(\hat{B}_i') = -\frac{aN_i^B}{2(N_i^B + M_i^B)} = -\frac{a}{2(1 + R_B)} \tag{6.30}$$

$$E(\hat{Y}_i^1) = E(\hat{A}_i') - E(\hat{B}_i) = \frac{aN_i^A}{2(N_i^A + M_i^A)} = \frac{a}{2(1 + R_A)} \tag{6.31}$$

$$\text{Var}(\hat{Y}_i^0) = \text{Var}(\hat{A}_i) + \text{Var}(\hat{B}_i') \leq \frac{T^2}{6(N_i + M_i)} = \frac{T^2}{6N_i(1 + R)} \tag{6.32}$$

$$\text{Var}(\hat{Y}_i^1) = \text{Var}(\hat{A}_i') + \text{Var}(\hat{B}_i) \leq \frac{T^2}{6(N_i + M_i)} = \frac{T^2}{6N_i(1 + R)} \tag{6.33}$$

Here $R_A = \frac{M_i^A}{N_i^A}, R_B = \frac{M_i^B}{N_i^B}, R = \frac{M_i}{N_i}$, and they represent the ratio between the number of chaff packets and the number of original packets in all time intervals assigned for watermark bit i. By the law of large number, $R_A \approx R_B \approx R$ when N_i is large.

After the chaff packets have been added to the watermarked packet flow, $\Pr[\hat{Y}_i^1 < 0]$ is the probability that an encoded bit '1' is mistakenly decoded as bit '0', and $\Pr[\hat{Y}_i^0 > 0]$ is the probability that an encoded bit '0' is mistakenly decoded as bit '1'.

Now we establish an upper bound on the watermark decoding error probability by applying the Chebyshev inequality to $\hat{Y}_i^0$ and $\hat{Y}_i^1$.

$$
\begin{aligned}
\Pr[\hat{Y}_i^0 > 0] &= \Pr[\hat{Y}_i^0 - E(\hat{Y}_i^0) > -E(\hat{Y}_i^0)] \\
&= \frac{1}{2}\Pr[|\hat{Y}_i^0 - E(\hat{Y}_i^0)| \geq -E(\hat{Y}_i^0)] \\
&\leq \frac{\mathrm{Var}(\hat{Y}_i^0)}{2(E(\hat{Y}_i^0))^2} \\
&= \frac{(1 + R_B)^2 T^2}{3a^2 N_i(1 + R)}
\end{aligned}
\tag{6.34}
$$

$$
\begin{aligned}
\Pr[\hat{Y}_i^1 < 0] &= \Pr[\hat{Y}_i^1 - E(\hat{Y}_i^1) < -E(\hat{Y}_i^1)] \\
&= \frac{1}{2}\Pr[|\hat{Y}_i^1 - E(\hat{Y}_i^1)| \geq E(\hat{Y}_i^1)] \\
&\leq \frac{\mathrm{Var}(\hat{Y}_i^1)}{2(E(\hat{Y}_i^1))^2} \\
&= \frac{(1 + R_A)^2 T^2}{3a^2 N_i(1 + R)}
\end{aligned}
\tag{6.35}
$$

Equations 6.34 and 6.35 show that bigger R_A, R_B, R would result higher upper bound of the decoding error probabilities. This analytical result confirms our intuition: the more chaff compared to the original packets, the more error the watermark decoding tends to have. However, no matter how big the R_A, R_B, R could be (as long as they are finite), we can always make the upper bound of the decoding error probabilities arbitrarily close to zero by having sufficiently large N_i. From Eq. 6.5, we can make N_i sufficiently large by having sufficiently large n_t, which is the number of packets in all time intervals that have been assigned for encoding/decoding each watermark bit. For a sufficiently long flow with sufficient packets, this can be easily done by increasing the redundancy r.

6.3 Fundamental Limitations of Adding Chaff and Cover Traffic

The analysis in Sect. 6.2.4.1 proves that interval centroid-based watermarking scheme can achieve asymptotic error-free watermark decoding even if the number of chaff packets added is many times more than the number of original packets, as long as the original flow is long enough and has enough packets. Furthermore, this analytical property holds true regardless of distribution of the chaff added. Once we can decode the unique watermark from the watermarked packet flow, the watermarked packet flow becomes uniquely identifiable. This result directly counters the claim by Blum et al. [8] "when the attacker can insert chaff that is more than a certain threshold fraction, the attacker can make the attacking streams mimic two independent random processes, and thus completely evade any detection algorithm."

Yu et al. [68] developed a different flow watermark scheme based direct sequence spread spectrum (DSSS) signal modulation. Their analysis shows that digital filters (i.e., high-pass filter, low-pass filter) can be used to recover the embedded watermark despite noises caused by chaff. Their result is consistent with our analytical result in Sect. 6.2.4.1. Works [34, 39] also demonstrate that watermark-based approach is able to correlate encrypted packet flows in the presence of both chaff and timing perturbation.

Besides analysis, we have empirically validated the impact of chaff over the decoding of our centroid based flow watermarking scheme. We have been able to reliably recover the watermark from the watermarked flow mixed with chaff that is 100 times more than the original packets provided the packet flow is long enough and has enough packets.

Blum et al. [8] has proved the hardness result in the presence of passive adversary who observes and analyzes the inter-packet timing characteristics passively without any active perturbation on the inter-packet timing. Despite their claim "hardness analysis will apply even when the monitor can actively manipulate the timing delay," the claimed hardness result has never been proved for scenarios with active adversary who actively perturb the inter-packet timing. On the other hand, our centroid based flow watermarking [63] and DSSS-based flow marking [68] have proved that the hardness result by work [8] is false in the presence of active adversary who can actively perturb the inter-packet timing.

This indicates that active adversary is fundamentally more powerful than passive adversary in term of capability in breaking anonymity.

From information theory's point of view, unless the low-latency anonymity system can completely eliminate the timing correlation between the original packet flow and the anonymized packet flow, there will be mutual information thus covert channel in the timing domain between the original packet flow and the anonymized packet flow. Our centroid based flow watermarking and the DSSS based flow watermarking are (less than optimal) coding schemes for the communication over the inter-packet timing based covert channel.

While adding chaff or cover traffic will decrease the mutual information in the timing domain, both our centroid based flow watermarking and DSSS based flow watermarking have proved that adding chaff or cover traffic will not eliminate the mutual information between the original packet flow and the anonymized packet flow. Therefore, adding chaff or cover traffic can not prevent us from recovering the watermark encoded in the inter-packet domain of a sufficiently long packet flow. This allows us to uniquely identify the anonymized packet flow thus break the anonymity completely. In other words, adding chaff or cover traffic is fundamentally limited in providing anonymity to long packet flows.

In the next section, we analyze the fundamental limitation of timing perturbation in providing anonymity to long packet flows.

6.4   Fundamental Limitation of Timing Perturbation

Timing perturbation directly interferes the inter-packet timing characteristics of any packet flow, and it causes error in decoding the watermark from the inter-packet timing domain. Assume all the information needed for encoding and decoding the watermark (i.e., tuple $< o, T, , IRNG, s >$) is unknown to the adversary, we use information theoretic analysis to reveal some fundamental limitation of the negative impact of the adversary's timing perturbation.

First, we identify the minimum brute force distortion required for the adversary to completely eliminate the encoded watermark and the optimal strategy to do so. We then investigate the extra constraints imposed by real-time communication and their implications to the adversary's capability of eliminating the watermark. We demonstrate that the real-time constraints make a fundamental difference in the adversary's capability. While the adversary is able to completely eliminate any encoded watermark from its carrier or host signal offline with sufficiently large distortion, he is not able to completely eliminate the encoded watermark from a general packet flow in real-time even with arbitrarily large but finite distortion.

6.4.1   Minimum Brute Force Perturbation Needed to Completely Remove Watermark

We use one random variable to model the time stamp of one packet, and a n-dimension vector of random variables to model a given packet flow of $n > 0$ packets. Let $S^N = < S_1, \ldots, S_N >$ (where $S_i \in R^+$ is a random variable) be the host signal (i.e., time stamp of original packet flow) to which some watermark will be encoded. Encoding a watermark into S^N will turn it into a slightly different (i.e., watermarked) signal $X^N = < X_1, \ldots, X_N >$ (where $X_i \in R^+$ is a random variable). The adversary could distort the watermarked signal X^N into another signal

$Y^N =< Y_1, \ldots, Y_N >$ (where $Y_i \in R^+$ is a random variable). Here we can use the *mean squared error* $MSE(X_i, Y_i) = E[(X_i - Y_i)^2]$ to measure the distortion between random variables X_i and Y_i. The overall distortion between X^N and Y^N can be measured by $D(X^N, Y^N) = \frac{1}{N} \sum_{i=1}^{N} MSE(X_i, Y_i)$.

We first analyze the distortion between single random variable X_i and Y_i. From the information-theoretic point of view, completely eliminating the watermark encoded in X_i from Y_i means eliminating the mutual information $I(X_i; Y_i)$ between X_i and Y_i. That is

$$I(X_i; Y_i) = H(X_i) - H(X_i|Y_i) = 0 \tag{6.36}$$

Then we have

$$H(X_i) = H(X_i|Y_i) = H(X_i, Y_i) - H(Y_i) \tag{6.37}$$

or

$$H(X_i, Y_i) = H(X_i) + H(Y_i) \tag{6.38}$$

No mutual information between X_i and Y_i means they are independent from each other. Thus the adversary needs to distort X_i into another independent random variable Y_i in order to completely remove any watermark encoded in X_i from Y_i.

Let $p(x_i, y_i)$ be the joint probability density function for random variables X_i and Y_i, and $p(x_i)$, $p(y_i)$ be the probability density functions for X_i and Y_i respectively. Then the mean square error between two independent random variables X_i and Y_i is

$$MSE(X_i, Y_i) \tag{6.39}$$
$$= E[(X_i - Y_i)^2]$$
$$= \int \int (x_i - y_i)^2 p(x_i, y_i) dx_i dy_i$$
$$= \int \int (x_i - y_i)^2 p(x_i) p(y_i) dx_i dy_i$$
$$= \int \int x_i^2 p(x_i) p(y_i) dx_i dy_i + \int \int y_i^2 p(x_i) p(y_i) dx_i dy_i - 2 \int \int x_i y_i p(x_i) p(y_i) dx_i dy_i$$
$$= \int x_i^2 p(x_i) dx_i + \int y_i^2 p(y_i) dy_i - 2 \int x_i p(x_i) dx_i \int y_i p(y_i) dy_i$$
$$= E(X_i^2) + E(Y_i^2) - 2E(X_i)E(Y_i)$$
$$= E(X_i^2) - E^2(X_i) + E(Y_i^2) - E^2(Y_i) + (E(X_i) - E(Y_i))^2$$
$$= Var(X_i) + Var(Y_i) + (E(X_i) - E(Y_i))^2$$

Here both $Var(Y_i)$ and $(E(X_i) - E(Y_i))^2$ are non-negative, and they will be zero only when Y_i equals the constant value $E(X_i)$.

Assume X_i is not a constant, then the minimum mean square error needed to convert one random variable X_i into another independent random variable Y_i is $Var(X_i)$, and it only occurs when Y_i equals constant value $E(X_i)$. Therefore, the minimum distortion required to completely eliminate any hidden information from any non-constant random variable X_i via brute force is $Var(X_i)$, and the optimal strategy to do so is to convert X_i into constant value $E(X_i)$.

The overall distortion $D(X^N, Y^N)$ between two n-dimensional vectors X^N and Y^N will reach its minimum $\frac{1}{N} \sum_{i=1}^{N} Var(X_i)$ when each $MSE(X_i, Y_i)$ reaches its minimum. Therefore, the optimal strategy to completely eliminate hidden information from X^N is to convert $X^N = < X_1, \ldots, X_N >$ into $Y^N = < E(X_1), \ldots, E(X_N) >$. In this case, Y^N is fixed regardless of the exact values of X^N, and there is zero mutual information between X^N and Y^N. This result holds true regardless of the distribution of each X_i in X^N.

This analytical result is consistent with Moulin's analysis [29, 30] regarding the achievable capacity of any information hiding scheme in the presence of distortion by an adversary. Moulin showed that the information hiding capacity for a normally distributed host signal would become zero once the distortion by the adversary becomes no less than the variance of the host signal. Here we have shown that distorting a host signal to the constant mean value is the optimal strategy, in term of minimum distortion needed, to completely eliminate any hidden information from the host signal.

6.4.2   Real-Time Constraints and Their Implications to the Adversary

We have shown that once the distortion reaches the level of the variance of the host signal, it is possible to completely remove any encoded information from the host signal offline. Now we consider the constraints imposed by real-time communication and investigate their implication to the adversary who is trying remove the encoded information from a given packet flow.

Given a real-time packet flow $P_1, \ldots, P_n$ with time stamps $t_1, \ldots, t_n$ respectively, the host signal in the inter-packet timing domain can be represented by $S^N = < t_1, \ldots, t_n >$. For simplicity, we assume there is no packet dropped during the transmission.[1] The real-time communication requirement imposes the following constraints on any distortions over the packet timing.

---

[1]In case there are packets dropped, we only consider those packets received and the corresponding packets sent.

1. Each packet can only be delayed.
2. The delay of each packet is bounded and finite, otherwise the real-time communication is broken.
3. The exact delay of packet P_k ($1 \leq k < n$) must be determined and executed before receiving all n packets, otherwise the delay of P_k is unbounded when $n \to \infty$.

We use δ_i to denote the delay added to packet P_i, then the distorted time stamp of packet P_i is $t'_i = t_i + \delta_i$. $I_i = t_{i+1} - t_i$ and $I'_i = t'_{i+1} - t'_i$ represent the original and distorted inter-packet delays (IPD) or inter-packet arrival time between P_{i+1} and P_i respectively. Then we have

$$\delta_k = t'_k - t_k = \delta_1 + \sum_{i=1}^{k-1}(I'_i - I_i) \tag{6.40}$$

It is easy to see that the original and the distorted inter-packet timing characteristics of packet flow $P_1, \ldots, P_n$ can be represented exactly by $< t_1, I_1, \ldots, I_{n-1} >$ and $< t'_1, I'_1, \ldots, I'_{n-1} >$ respectively.

According to the results in Sect. 6.4.1, in order to completely eliminate any information encoded in the original inter-packet timing signal $< t_1, I_1, \ldots, I_{n-1} >$, the adversary has to disturb $< t_1, I_1, \ldots, I_{n-1} >$ into a completely independent signal $< I'_1, \ldots, I'_{n-1} >$. Therefore, the distorted pattern $< I'_1, \ldots, I'_{n-1} >$ is essentially pre-determined without the exact knowledge of the original inter-packet timing characteristics $< t_1, I_1, \ldots, I_{n-1} >$. This means that the adversary has to determine $< I'_1, \ldots, I'_{n-1} >$ before he ever knows $< t_1, I_1, \ldots, I_{n-1} >$. However, the adversary could buffer some packets before determining the exact delay of the first packet δ_1.

Intuitively, the real-time constraints limit how much the adversary can buffer. Let $D > 0$ be the arbitrarily large but finite maximum delay that could be added to any packet, and let I_{min} and I_{max} be the minimum and the maximum of all I_i's respectively. Then, the adversary could buffer at most $\frac{D}{I_{min}}$ packets before determining and applying the exact delay δ_1 to packet P_1. Assume the adversary buffers b ($0 < b < n$) packets: $P_1, \ldots, P_b$ before he determines the exact value of δ_1, from Eq. (6.40), we have

$$\delta_n = \delta_b + \sum_{i=b}^{n-1}(I'_i - I_i) \tag{6.41}$$

From the real-time constraint $\delta_n \in [0, D]$, we have

$$-\frac{\delta_b}{n-b} \leq \frac{1}{n-b}\sum_{i=b}^{n-1} I'_i - \frac{1}{n-b}\sum_{i=b}^{n-1} I_i \leq \frac{D - \delta_b}{n-b} \tag{6.42}$$

Because both δ_b and D are fixed and finite, we have

$$\lim_{n \to \infty} \frac{1}{n-b} \sum_{i=b}^{n-1} I_i' = \lim_{n \to \infty} \frac{1}{n-b} \sum_{i=b}^{n-1} I_i \qquad (6.43)$$

Therefore, after the first b packets, the real-time constraints require the average inter-packet arrival time (or equivalently the average packet rate) of the perturbed packet flow to be arbitrarily close to that of the original packet flow with sufficiently large n. On the other hand, in order to completely eliminate any information encoded in the inter-packet timing of a given packet flow, the adversary has to determine an independent $< I_b', \ldots, I_{n-1}' >$ before he knows $< I_b, \ldots, I_{n-1} >$.

When $I_{min} < I_{max}$ and n is large, it is impossible for the adversary to know the exact average inter-packet arrival time $\frac{1}{n-b} \sum_{i=b}^{n-1} I_i (I_i \in [I_{min}, I_{max}])$ before he knows $< I_b, \ldots, I_{n-1} >$. Therefore, it is impossible for the adversary to determine an independent $< I_b', \ldots, I_{n-1}' >$ with an average inter-packet arrival time arbitrarily close to some unknown average inter-packet arrival time $\frac{1}{n-b} \sum_{i=b}^{n-1} I_i$ of some unreceived packets flow $P_{b+1}, \ldots, P_n$.

Therefore, it is impossible for the adversary to meet all the real-time constraints while he tries to completely eliminate all the encoded information from the inter-packet timing domain of a given packet flow whose inter-packet arrival time is not a constant (i.e., $I_{max} > I_{min}$). In other words, it is generally infeasible for the adversary to completely eliminate all the information encoded in the inter-packet timing domain in real-time from a sufficiently long packet flow even with arbitrarily large delays.

Chapter 7
Conclusion

While traceback and anonymity are important issues in network security, their goals are exactly opposite. Therefore, effective traceback techniques impose challenges in achieving anonymity and vice versa. Recognizing this inherent connection between traceback and anonymity, we have presented recent research results in both traceback and anonymity with emphasis on how they interact with each other.

7.1 Summary

Encryption has long been used as a building block for achieving anonymity. At the same time, it prevents traceback from correlating traffic based on content. To track encrypted traffic, researchers have developed inter-packet timing based approaches that have been shown to be effective in correlating encrypted traffic. Such inter-packet timing based correlation becomes the timing attack on anonymity and renders encryption alone ineffective in achieving anonymity.

To counter the timing attack against anonymity, researcher have proposed various transformations to interfere the inter-packet timing. Specifically, timing perturbation, adding chaff (i.e., cover traffic or bogus packets), flow mixing are indispensable building blocks of low-latency anonymity systems. It has been shown that both timing perturbation and chaff are effective against passive timing attack which do not change the inter-packet timing. In other words, the state of the art anonymity systems are robust against passive timing attack.

Active timing attack, on the other hand, can actively perturb the inter-packet timing. Specifically, flow watermarking schemes can embed a unique signal (i.e., some random bit string) into the inter-packet timing of packet flows by delaying selected packets. Researches have shown that flow watermarking can reliably and uniquely identify a sufficiently long watermarked flow in the presence of combinations of almost all existing low-latency anonymity techniques such as chaff, flow mixing and

© The Author(s) 2015
X. Wang, D. Reeves, *Traceback and Anonymity*, SpringerBriefs
in Computer Science, DOI 10.1007/978-1-4939-3441-6_7

timing perturbation. Therefore, active timing attack is fundamentally more powerful than passive timing attack. From information theoretic point of view, active timing attack (e.g., flow watermarking) essentially exploits the covert channel in the inter-packet timing domain. Due to the real-time constraint, it is generally impossible to completely eliminate the mutual information from the inter-packet timing based covert channel of a sufficiently long packet flow. Therefore, active timing attack is always applicable to all sufficiently long packet flows and existing low-latency anonymity systems are fundamentally limited in achieving anonymity.

7.2   Open Problems and Future Works

We have shown that there are close interaction and trade off between traceback and anonymity techniques. The exact level of traceback and anonymity we can achieve depends on better techniques to be developed in the future. From information and coding theoretic points of view, existing flow watermarking schemes are far from optimal in that the bandwidths of corresponding covert channels are well below the Shannon limit. Therefore, there exist better and more effective flow watermarking schemes that will result more effective traceback. On the other hand, There are likely better ways to achieve better anonymity. For example, there could exist better timing perturbation strategies and better chaff strategies that are more effective in anonymizing a given packet flow under given constraints.

Currently, we do not know exactly (1) to what extent traceback techniques can recover the path and the source of anonymized packet flow in the presence of all possible anonymity techniques; and (2) to what extent we can anonymize a given network flow given all possible traceback techniques. However, we believe there exists certain fundamental limit on the level of traceback and anonymity we can ultimately achieve.

In order to figure out such a fundamental limit in achieving traceback and anonymity, we need to be able to analyze quantitatively and rigorously. At least, we need some more general and accurate metrics to measure and represent the signal to noise ratio (SNR) in the context of traceback and anonymity. Such a metric would enable us to compare different traceback, anonymity techniques quantitatively and fairly.

Despite the close interaction between the traceback and anonymity techniques, existing researches tend to approach each of these issues separately and independently. We hope our work helps bridge the gap between these two inherently related research areas, and motivates research that treats traceback and anonymity as two sides of one technical problem.

References

1. Cypherpunk. http://en.wikipedia.org/wiki/Cypherpunk
2. Number of Internet Hosts. http://ftp.isc.org/www/survey/reports/current/
3. The Anonymizer. http://anonymizer.com
4. A.C. Snoeren, C. Partridge, L.A. Sanchez, C.E. Jone, F. Tchakountio, S.T. Kent, W.T. Strayer, Hash-based IP traceback, in *Proceedings of ACM SIGCOMM 2001*, San Diego, Nov 2001, pp. 3–14
5. J.P. Anderson, Computer Security Threat Monitoring and Surveillance. Technical Report, James P. Anderson Co., Fort Washington, Apr 1980
6. A. Beimel, S. Dolev, Buses for anonymous message delivery. J. Cryptol. **16**(1), 25–39 (2003)
7. O. Berthold, H. Federrath, S. Köpsell, Web MIXes: a system for anonymous and unobservable internet access, in *Proceedings of Designing Privacy Enhancing Technologies: Workshop on Design Issues in Anonymity and Unobservability*, Berkeley, July 2000, pp. 115–129
8. A. Blum, D. Song, S. Venkataraman, Detection of interactive stepping stones: algorithms and confidence bounds, in *Proceedings of the 7th International Symposium on Recent Advances in Intrusion Detection (RAID 2004)*, Sophia-Antipolis, Sept 2004, pp. 258–277
9. B. Carrier, C. Shields, A recursive session token protocol for use in computer forensics and TCP traceback, in *Proceedings of Proceedings of the 21th Annual Joint Conference of the IEEE Computer and Communications Societies (Infocom 2002)*, New York, Apr 2002, pp. 1540–1546
10. D. Chaum, Untraceable electronic mail, return addresses, and digital pseudonyms. Commun. ACM **24**(2), 84–88 (1981)
11. D. Chaum, The dining cryptographers problem: unconditional sender and recipient untraceability. J. Cryptol. **1**(1), 65–75 (1988)
12. D. Chaum, E.V. Heyst, Group signatures, in *Proceedings of the 1991 Workshop on the Theory and Application of Cryptographic Techniques on Advances in Cryptology (EUROCRYPT 1991)*, Brighton, Apr 1991, pp. 257–265
13. I.J. Cox, M.L. Miller, J.A. Bloom, *Digital Watermarking* (Morgan-Kaufmann, San Francisco, 2002)
14. G. Danezis, R. Dingledine, N. Mathewson, Mixminion: design of a type III anonymous remailer protocol, in *Proceedings of the 2003 IEEE Symposium on Security and Privacy (S&P 2003)*, Berkeley, May 2003, pp. 183–195
15. D. Dean, M. Franklin, A. Stubblefield, An algebraic approach to IP traceback. ACM Trans. Inf. Syst. Secur. (TISSEC) **5**(2):119–137 (2002)
16. M.H. deGroot, *Probability and Statistics* (Addison-Wesley, Reading, 1989)

© The Author(s) 2015   77
X. Wang, D. Reeves, *Traceback and Anonymity*, SpringerBriefs
in Computer Science, DOI 10.1007/978-1-4939-3441-6

17. R. Dingledine, N. Mathewson, P. Syverson, Tor: the second-generation onion routing, in *Proceedings of the 13th USENIX Security Symposium*, San Diego, Aug 2004, pp. 303–320. USENIX

18. D.L. Donoho, A.G. Flesia, U. Shankar, V. Paxson, J. Coit, S. Staniford, Multiscale stepping stone detection: detecting pairs of jittered interactive streams by exploiting maximum tolerable delay, in *Proceedings of the 5th International Symposium on Recent Advances in Intrusion Detection (RAID 2002)*, Zurich, Oct 2002, pp. 17–35

19. M.J. Freedman, R. Morris, Tarzan: a peer-to-peer anonymizing network layer, in *Proceedings of the 9th ACM Conference on Computer and Communications Security (CCS 2002)*, Washington, DC, Nov 2002, pp. 193–206

20. M.T. Goodrich, Efficient packet marking for large-scale IP traceback, in *Proceedings of the 9th ACM Conference on Computer and Communications Security (CCS 2002)*, Washington, DC, Nov 2002, pp. 117–126

21. Y. Guan, X. Fu, D. Xuan, P.U. Shenoy, R. Bettati, W. Zhao, Netcamo: camouflaging network traffic for qosguaranteed. IEEE Trans. Syst. Man Cybern. **34**(4), 253–265 (2001)

22. L.T. Heberlein, K. Levitt, B. Mukherjee, Internetwork security monitor: an intrusion-detection system for large-scale networks, in *Proceedings of the 15th National Computer Security Conference*, Baltimore, Oct 1992

23. S. Helmers, A Brief History of anon.penet.fi – The Legendary Anonymous Remailer. http://www.december.com/cmc/mag/1997/sep/helmers.html

24. H.T. Jung, H.L. Kim, Y.M. Seo, G. Choe, S. Min, C.S. Kim, K. Koh, Caller identification system in the internet environment, in *Proceedings of the 4th USENIX Security Symposium*, Santa Clara, Aug 1993, pp. 69–78

25. S. Kent, K. Seo, Security architecture for the internet protocol, *RFC 4301*, IETF, Dec 2005

26. D. Kesdogan, D. Agrawal, V. Pham, D. Agrawal, Fundamental limits on the anonymity provided by the MIX technique, in *Proceedings of the 2006 IEEE Symposium on Security & Privacy (S&P 2006)*, Oakland, May 2006, pp. 86–99

27. B.N. Levine, M.K. Reiter, C. Wang, M.K. Wright, Timing attacks in low-latency mix-based systems, in *Proceedings of Financial Cryptography (FC '04)*, ed. by A. Juels. LNCS, vol. 3110 (Springer, Berlin/Heidelberg, 2004), pp. 251–265

28. U. Moeller, L. Cottrell, P. Palfrader, L. Sassaman, Mixmaster Protocol Version 2. *Internet-Draft*, IETF, Dec 2004

29. P. Moulin, Information-hiding games, in *Proceedings of International Workshop on Digital Watermarking (IWDW 2003)*, Seoul, May 2003, pp. 82–91

30. P. Moulin, J.A. O'Sullivan, Information-theoretic analysis of information hiding. IEEE Trans. Inf. Theory **49**(3), 563–593 (2003)

31. R. Oppliger, Internet security: firewalls and beyond. Commun. ACM **40**(5), 92–102 (1997)

32. L. Øverlier, P. Syverson, Locating hidden servers, in *Proceedings of the 2006 IEEE Symposium on Security & Privacy (S&P 2006)*, Oakland, May 2006, pp. 100–114

33. K. Park, H. Lee, On the effectiveness of probabilistic packet marking for IP traceback under denial of service attack, in *Proceedings of the 20th Annual Joint Conference of the IEEE Computer and Communications Societies (Infocom 2001)*, Anchorage, Apr 2001, pp. 338–347

34. P. Peng, P. Ning, D.S. Reeves, X. Wang, Active timing-based correlation of perturbed traffic flows with chaff packets, in *Proceedings of the 2nd International Workshop on Security in Distributed Computing Systems (SDCS-2005)*, Columbus, Ohio, USA, June 2005, pp. 107–113

35. A. Pfitzmann, M. Hansen, A terminology for talking about privacy by data minimization: anonymity, unlinkability, undetectability, unobservability, pseudonymity, and identity management, 2010. http://dud.inf.tu-dresden.de/literatur/Anon_Terminology_v0.34.pdf

36. B. Pfitzmann, A. Pfizmann, How to break the direct RSA-implementation of mixes, in *Proceedings of the 1989 Workshop on the Theory and Application of Cryptographic Techniques on Advances in Cryptology (EUROCRYPT 1989)*, Houthalen, Apr 1989, pp. 373–381

37. B. Prince, Attackers Adopt 'Advanced Evasion Techniques' to Beat IPS. http://securitywatch. eweek.com/intrusion_detectionprevention/attackers_adopt_advanced_evasion_techniques_ beat_ips.html

38. Y. Pyun, D.S. Reeves, Deployment of network monitors for attack attribution, in *Proceedings of the Fourth International Conference on Broadband Communications, Networks, and Systems (IEEE Broadnets 2007)*, Raleigh, Sept 2007, pp. 525–534

39. Y.J. Pyun, Y.H. Park, X. Wang, D.S. Reeves, P. Ning, Tracing traffic through intermediate hosts that repacketize flows, in *Proceedings of the 26th Annual IEEE Conference on Computer Communications (Infocom 2007)*, Anchorage, May 2007. IEEE

40. F. Rashid, Dutch CA Files for Bankruptcy After Security Breach. http://securitywatch.eweek. com/infrastructure_security/dutch_ca_files_for_bankruptcy_after_security_breach.html

41. F. Rashid, Hackers Target Bankers' Personal Data as Part of "Occupy Wall Street". http://securitywatch.eweek.com/hactivism/hackers_target_bankers_personal_data_ as_part_of_occupy_wall_street.html

42. F. Rashid, McAfee Predicts More Hacktivism in 2012. http://securitywatch.eweek.com/ hactivism/mcafee_predicts_more_hacktivism_in_2012.html

43. F. Rashid, NASA Repeatedly Attacked, Jet Propulsion Lab Compromised. http:// securitywatch.eweek.com/data_breach/nasa_repeatedly_attacked_jet_propulsion_lab_ compromised.html

44. F. Rashid, Sony PSN Hackers Used Amazon EC2 in Attack. http://securitywatch.eweek.com/ data_breach/sony_psn_hackers_used_amazon_ec2_in_attack.html

45. M.G. Reed, P.F. Syverson, D.M. Goldschlag, Anonymous connections and onion routing. IEEE JSAC Copyr. Priv. Prot. **16**(4), 482–494 (1998)

46. M. Reiter, A. Rubin, Crowds: anonymity for web transactions. ACM TISSEC **1**(1), 66–92 (1998)

47. M. Rennhard, B. Plattner, Introducing MorphMix: peer-to-peer based anonymous internet usage with collusion detection, in *Proceedings of the 2002 ACM Workshop on Privacy in the Electronic Society (WPES 2002)*, Washington, DC, Nov 2002, pp. 91–102

48. R.L. Rivest, A. Shamir, Y. Tauman, How to leak a secret, in *Proceedings of the 7th International Conference on the Theory and Application of Cryptology and Information Security: Advances in Cryptology (ASIACRYPT 2001)* (Springer, Berlin/Heidelberg, 2001), pp. 554–567

49. S. Savage, D. Wetherall, A. Karlin, T. Anderson, Practical network support for IP traceback, in *Proceedings of ACM SIGCOMM 2000*, Stockholm, Sept 2000, pp. 295–306

50. D. Schnackenberg, K. Djahandari, D. Strene, Infrastructure for intrusion detection and response, in *Proceedings of the 2000 DARPA Information Survivability Conference and Exposition (DISCEX 2000)*, Hilton Head, 2000, pp. 3–11

51. R. Sherwood, B. Bhattacharjee, A. Srinivasan, P5: a protocol for scalable anonymous communication, in *Proceedings of 2002 IEEE Symposium on Security and Privacy (S&P 2002)*, Oakland, May 2002

52. C. Shields, B.N. Levine, A protocol for anonymous communication over the internet, in *Proceedings of the 7th ACM Conference on Computer and Communications Security (CCS 2000)*, Athens, Nov 2000, pp. 33–42

53. S.R. Snapp, J. Brentano, G.V. Dias, T.L. Goan, L.T. Heberlein, C. lin Ho, K.N. Levitt, B. Mukherjee, S.E. Smaha, T. Grance, D.M. Teal, D. Mansur, DIDS (distributed intrusion detection system) – motivation, architecture, and an early prototype, in *Proceedings of the 14th National Computer Security Conference*, Baltimore, 1991, pp. 167–176

54. D. Song, A. Perrig, Advanced and authenticated marking scheme for IP traceback, in *Proceedings of the 20th Annual Joint Conference of the IEEE Computer and Communications Societies (Infocom 2001)*, Anchorage, Apr 2001, pp. 878–886

55. S. Staniford-Chen, L.T. Heberlein, Holding intruders accountable on the internet, in *Proceedings of the 1995 IEEE Symposium on Security & Privacy (S&P 1995)*, Oakland, May 1995, pp. 39–49

56. C. Stoll, *The Cuckoo's Egg: Tracking Spy Through the Maze of Computer Espionage* (Pocket Books, New York, 1990)
57. P. Tabriz, N. Borisov, Breaking the collusion detection mechanism of morphmix, in *Proceedings of the 6th International Conference on Privacy Enhancing Technologies (PET 2006)*, Cambridge, June 2006, pp. 368–383
58. C.E.R. Team, CERT Advisory CA-96.21: CERT Advisory TCP SYN Flooding and IP Spoofing Attacks. http://www.cert.org/advisories/CA-96.21.tcp_syn_flooding.html
59. C.E.R. Team, CERT Advisory CA-96.26: Denial-of-Service Attack via Pings. http://www.cert.org/advisories/CA-96.26.ping.html
60. C.E.R. Team, CERT Advisory CA-98.01: CERT Advisory "smurf" IP Denial-of-Service. http://www.cert.org/advisories/CA-98.01.smurf.html
61. P. Venkitasubramaniam, L. Tong, Anonymous networking with minimum latency in multihop networks, in *Proceedings of the 2008 IEEE Symposium on Security & Privacy (S&P 2008)*, Oakland, May 2008, pp. 18–32
62. R. Walters, Cyber Attacks on U.S. Companies in 2014, 2014. http://www.heritage.org/research/reports/2014/10/cyber-attacks-on-us-companies-in-2014
63. X. Wang, S. Chen, S. Jajodia, Network flow watermarking attack on low-latency anonymous communication systems, in *Proceedings of the 2007 IEEE Symposium on Security & Privacy (S&P 2007)*, Oakland, May 2007, pp. 116–130
64. X. Wang, D.S. Reeves, S.F. Wu, Inter-packet delay based correlation for tracing encrypted connections through stepping stones, in *Proceedings of the 7th European Symposium on Research in Computer Security (ESORICS 2002)*, Zurich, Oct 2002, pp. 244–263
65. X. Wang, D.S. Reeves, S.F. Wu, J. Yuill, Sleepy watermark tracing: an active network-based intrusion response framework, in *Proceedings of the 16th International Conference on Information Security (IFIP/Sec 2001)*, Paris, June 2001, pp. 369–384
66. T. Ylonen, C. Lonvick, The Secure Shell (SSH) Protocol Architecture. *RFC 4251*, IETF, Jan 2006
67. K. Yoda, H. Etoh, Finding a connection chain for tracing intruders, in *Proceedings of the 6th European Symposium on Research in Computer Security (ESORICS 2000)*, Toulouse, Oct 2000, pp. 191–205
68. W. Yu, X. Fu, S. Graham, D. Xuan, W. Zhao, DSSS-based flow marking technique for invisible traceback, in *Proceedings of the 2007 IEEE Symposium on Security & Privacy (S&P 2007)*, Oakland, May 2007, pp. 18–32
69. Y. Zhang, V. Paxson, Detecting stepping stones, in *Proceedings of the 9th USENIX Security Symposium*, Denver, Aug 2000, pp. 171–184

Printed in the United States
By Bookmasters